Who are You?

WHO ARE YOU?

Identity in Christ

David Rocha

PARAKLETOS PUBLISHING
MODESTO

DEDICATION

This book is dedicated, first of all, to my Lord and Savior, Jesus Christ. Secondly, to my beautiful wife Sharon and our children and grandchildren. Also to my parents Robert and Erminia Rocha and family. I love you all. Thank you to all that receive this teaching; God bless you.

CONTENTS

CREDITS

Photography: Sharon Mendoza Rocha
Cover and back design: David Rocha
www.houseofrestchurch.com

FOREWORD BY CARLOS GARCIA

"Drug Addict."
This used to be my identity.

In hindsight, I've come to learn that I was so much more than just a "drug addict," I was a person first and foremost. I was a person that struggled with substance abuse. I was a person trying to cover up the pain in my life. Seeing myself as a "drug addict" was a very narrow lens that confined me to a broken identity. This was just an extra layer of a broken identity that I adopted. Deep down inside, I thought of myself as a loser, a reject, a throwaway, and a whole lot of other negative descriptions. I had no purpose or direction in my life. Drugs helped numb the pain. My identity was rooted in being fatherless and not having someone speak into my life and tell me who I was as a young man. This left me in a place of figuring it out on my own, so I gleaned my identity from my peers at school, my culture, and my skewed understanding of who I thought God was and what this world was all about. It was a painful existence. Today I know different.

Today I know I am a child of God, created in His image, and my worth and value are rooted in who God says I am, not in who the world says that I am. It's a blessing to know that my identity isn't tied to my career, my giftings, how much money I make, my sin, my failures, my past experiences, or anything that I do. My identity is settled in the Word of God. The steady, rock-solid, unmovable, never-changing Word of God. Praise be to God! Because of the rock-solid foundation of God's Word. I'm able to build my life, not on the shifting sands of the culture and its ever-changing opinions, but God's Truth and God's purposes for my life. You can too.

In his insightful book 'Who are you?", Pastor David Rocha leads us on a journey of discovery, teaching us about the building blocks God uses to shape our true identity that is found only in Christ. If you ever wondered about why you were born and God's purpose for your life, this book will help you. You will find healing for your soul and gain insight into who God is, who God says you are, and what this means for your life. At the end of this book, you will better understand what the Bible is about and how it applies to the deepest part of who you are – Your identity.

I pray you are blessed as I was as you read this transformational book.

Carlos Garcia

1

WHERE IT ALL BEGAN WITH ME

I grew up in a Christian home filled with miracles. The first miracle I had personally witnessed was my dad, an alcoholic, surrendering his life to Jesus. From that moment on, my dad changed. I was five years old when my mom gave her life to the Lord, and she would take me to church with her each Sunday. She was pregnant with my little brother Angel. For the next three years, I saw my mother cry and pray for my dad to stop drinking. He was a functioning alcoholic, which meant that he always paid the bills and kept us fed. But they were now raising four sons, and my mom wanted a better example for us. The drinking over the years had progressed from socially drinking to getting home from work and drinking through the evening. My mom would share the gospel with him, and at times, he would tolerate it, but he couldn't kick the habit. He would come into my room many nights, which I shared with my oldest brother, and I would hear him cry. He would stumble in drunk and promise that someday he would change. I always pretended to be asleep.

All of this changed when a visiting pastor preached at my mom's church. It was a small brick building in the downtown Stockton Ca, area. By this time, it had been three years since my mom had been saved. Once in a while, she would convince my dad to take her to church, hoping that it would move his heart. Then, on this day, the visiting pastor was finishing up the service. Then, when the preacher called the congregation to the altar, my dad knew service was almost over. He could already taste the tall can of beer he was about to buy on the drive back to Tracy. So as the pastor was praying for many, he looked to my dad, still sitting in his chair. My dad assumed the preacher was beckoning someone behind him. So he looked back, and there was nobody there.

The preacher then beckoned to my dad again and called him up. My dad had a choice. He could either ignore the preacher or inquire about what the preacher wanted. As my dad walked up to the altar area, the preacher asked a simple question. "Are you saved?" My dad was so tired of his addictions, so tired of not being able to change. He no longer wanted to lie to God. He shook his head that he was not saved. The preacher did not lead my dad in a sinners prayer or call everyone's attention to lay praying hands on him. It was no longer important that the preacher was standing there in front of my dad. This was a spiritual moment, a time that stood still. My dad was not answering the preacher; he was answering God. In his heart, he said to the Lord, "I am tired, and I can't change. I'm a drunk. I can't do this anymore." It was at that moment, in a little church building, that a miracle happened. Lightning did not fall from the sky; the Red Sea didn't part. But God miraculously changed the heart of my dad in an instant. It happened so fast that he didn't even realize what had happened. He never drank that beer after church, and that was the year 1980. The life of our family was never the same from that day forward. At that moment, I knew without a shadow of a doubt that God was real and that He still had the power to create miracles. I witnessed demon possession a handful of times as a child, and I saw them delivered and set free. These people would become a part of the church family throughout my childhood. I say this because I need to clarify that it wasn't just a random person I never saw again. They were possessed. I saw their facial features change, voices change and contort beyond human capabilities. Yet, they were set free and served God for the rest of their lives.

I also witnessed physical healing in my family. All of this can be debatable from a non-believers standpoint. But I will share what is not debatable, at least not in my mind. One day, when I was twelve, I woke up with a swollen cheek. My mom instantly called the dentist because the pain radiated from my jaw. It was excruciating, and all I could do was lay there and cry. The pain was like no other pain I have ever felt in my life. I was taken to our family dentist, and he did all he could to find out the problem. He did X-rays and an examination and could not find anything. The pain was worsening. I was sent home and told to rest. I got home and laid in bed in complete agony. The next day was worse than the day before. This time my mom took me back to the dentist, and he did a thorough examination once again. He was confused and decided to send me to a dental specialist in Stockton. Finally, I would be seen by an expert, and this pain would be relieved. On the drive to Stockton, I remember leaning my head on the window and crying. My dad was at work, so it was just my mom and me. Once again, the specialist found nothing. He did more tests than my family dentist and concluded that nothing was wrong with me. I was once again sent home with no relief from the pain. By this time, I hadn't eaten in two days, and my mom was distraught. She brought me home and laid me on her bed. She prayed for me, consoled me as a mother does. At times, she even cried with me; no mother wants to see their child in pain. When my dad got home from work, he was surprised that I was still in agony. He assumed that the specialist would find out what was wrong and that I would be better. I still remember hearing my mom feeding my dad his dinner after a long day of work. They both entered and prayed for me. This time the pain got worse. They went back to the dining room, and I could hear them talking. I couldn't take it anymore. I needed Jesus to heal me. I needed Jesus to do what He did in the stories of the Bible. I got up from the bed and walked over to the kitchen, and begged my dad to pray for me. He looked concerned, and once again, he and my mom prayed for me. This time the pain shot through my jaw to my brain like lightning. My dad looked frustrated, and I remember his eyes watering. He didn't know what to do as he walked away from me, defeated into his bedroom. I had my back against the refrigerator and slowly slid down in agony. As my dad walked into his bedroom, he was talking to God.

"Why won't you heal him. I don't know what to do." Suddenly my dad heard the voice of God. It was the first time he had ever heard God in that way. "Go back and pray for Him!" My dad did not hesitate. He came walking into the kitchen with powerful confidence. He had a look of determination that I had never seen in him. He said, "Get up!" and before I realized it, I was standing up. I can't remember what words my dad said, but I clearly remember what I felt. My eyes were closed, and I felt a hand reach from the top of my head into my jaw and pull something. I knew it was Jesus. As the hand pulled something up and out, the pain immediately left. From one second to the next, I was healed, completely. I cried and hugged my parents. My dad was just as astonished as me that God used him in such a way. This is something I will never forget. In those years, I saw many more healings and miracles.

By the time I was an adult, I had forgotten about the things of God. I was living life for myself and was living a criminal lifestyle. This is all described in my book 'Lost in the Storm.' At thirty-two, I surrendered my life to the Lord while in solitary confinement in federal prison. So long ago were the years of deliverance, healing, and miracles. I was reading my Bible and learning so much. I was leading my fellow inmates to the Lord and giving them Bible studies each day. Yet, I always felt that something was missing. I read a Bible where God spoke, yet I didn't hear His voice. I read about miracles, healing, and demons screaming in fear of Jesus. When one surrenders their life to the Lord and fails to see these things, we tend to build a belief system. Maybe those spiritual things were for the times of the Bible, or maybe God doesn't want to use me in this way. We make up all kinds of excuses because it's better than admitting to ourselves that we got it wrong. Over the years, I have realized that something is missing in much of Christianity. This is the reason for this book. I have taught this in seminars over the years, but I would say some things each time and not others. I realized that I needed to write it in book form and be as exhaustive as possible. The church needs to know who they truly are in Christ. This is the missing piece of the puzzle that many are looking for.

I have often said that nearly every Christian church denomination does a fantastic job at exalting Jesus. It does not matter which church; this is done well. I am not speaking about individual doctrines that differ from each denomination. I am simply talking about the truth of who God is, how glorious and holy He is, and especially how powerful He is. But what is not taught is how that relates to us. If we are only taught how exalted God is, this is only half of the truth. Yes, He is all of those things; this cannot be argued. Yet the more the church lifts the Lord, the farther He gets from us. This is why many new believers lose their fire. At the beginning of a recent convert, they feel as if Jesus is right there with them. But as they attend church, listen to Bible studies, they quickly begin to feel a disconnect. God is holy; we are worms. God is powerful; we are weak. God is majestic; we are sinners. This slowly causes the believer to doubt themselves, and once again, shame, guilt, and condemnation creep in. Jesus did save you to make you feel worse. The Bible says we can step into the throne room boldly. This book is foundational in helping you understand your rightful standing in Christ. Scripture says that we are in heavenly places in Christ Jesus. If He lives in us, then He is here on earth. And if we are hidden in Him, then we are with Him in heaven also. Please do not look at this book as just another tool in your belt. Allow the truth of who you are in Christ to draw you closer than you have ever been to your Lord and Savior. This is foundational in your life in Christ. He does not want you to feel far from Him. How effective can we ever truly be if we think this way? On the flip side of that coin, how effective can you be if you truly believed that He was standing with you in everything you said and did? This is the Christian the devil and his demons fear. One that knows who they are in Christ. We need to begin to renew our minds and finally see ourselves as who we truly are. Then and only then will we be able to destroy the works of the devil and demolish his strongholds.

2

CREATION

Let's begin. Before we dive deep into identity, we always need to go back to the beginning. We must start where it all began, in creation. I have always believed that this teaching is not something to be added to your repertoire of Christian beliefs and thoughts. It is foundational. It is an accurate way of seeing the Word of God and the Lord from past to present. That way, your foundation is solid and non-moving. When using this as foundational, everything else begins to line up and make sense, making a non-wobbly Christian life. Isn't that why we are here together? Because regardless of how long you've been serving God, something feels off. It feels like a piece of the puzzle is missing in your life in Christ. So let's go back to creation.

Creation itself is something to be thought about first. For many of you, this sounds like a topic you've heard and thought about a lot. For others, maybe you haven't given it enough thought. I know it sounds simple, but step number one is we all have to agree that God is the creator.

Genesis 1:1 says, '*in the beginning, God created the heavens and the earth.*'

It is of high importance that we establish this. There is only one creator. Satan is not a creator; neither is your pastor, favorite evangelist, your teacher, your favorite rapper, or the president is not a creator. Whoever it is that you look up to and are influenced by. They might be great in what they do, but they are not a creator. The bottom line is there is only one creator. In the beginning, God created. It is foundational. I might sound like I'm repeating myself, but we need to anchor this truth deep into our hearts. God created the heavens and the earth.

Let's look at another Bible scripture written in Genesis 2:4

This is the history of the heavens and the earth when they were created, in the day that the Lord God made the earth and the heavens

In reading this scripture, we see once again that

God is the creator of all things. Not only the things on earth but also the heavens. The galaxies, the universe. He created each planet and star. The earth does not even possess telescopes that can reach the furthest stars. So let's calibrate this thought into our heads. God is not just the God of the earth. He is the God of the cosmos. Not only is He the God of the universe, but He is also the creator of it all. I don't know about you, but that blows me away. It stretches my mind when I truly begin to think about a creator so powerful, artistic, intelligent, much less caring about us on this tiny blue planet called earth. It's mind-boggling. God does not compete with anyone. Everything besides God has been created. God was not created. He was and always will be. I know, I know. That makes your brain shake. So don't worry; it makes my brain shake also. Just the thought takes my breath away. So let's go back to the original foundational piece, God is the creator and the sole creator. There is nothing or no one else. Nothing exists that was not created by Him.

So now that we've established that God is the creator of all things, let's take a few minutes to talk about us. We have a minimal glimpse of the cosmos, life, and God. One instance is we are entirely confined by time. Many don't think of time as limiting, but it is very limiting. I'll prove it. Can you rewind your life to five minutes ago? Can you forward your life just a simple fifteen seconds? Of course, the answer is we cannot. No matter how much influence, education, or money you have. We live in the space of 'time.' Yet, God does not live in time.

Interestingly, our view of life is in 'time,' so we automatically assume that God sees things in 'time.' I'm positive God laughs when we try to confine Him to 'time.' If the planets in our solar system could speak, even they would laugh. Because our 'time' is limited to those on this earth. The only reason we can measure a twenty-four-hour day is that our planet is spinning. And once it turns a complete 360 rotation, we call that a day. So what happens if you are floating in space looking at the earth. What is a day to you? Simply leaving the planet, you are no longer confined to a twenty-four-hour day. Only on the earth is a clock or watch relevant.

Our view of life is through a timeline. We have a past, present, and future. Everything fits in the confines of our timeline. Yet, God does not work in time. So keep that thought in mind as we read a verse in the book of Hebrews 13:8

Jesus Christ, is the same yesterday, today, and forever.

According to this verse, Jesus is not subject to time. He does not exist in a world confined by linear timelines. This is important to establish now at the beginning of this book. The Lord, heavenly beings, and even demonic beings are not subject to time. Think about the disadvantage we humans are at with just that fact. Let's go even further; our true selves, our soul, are not subject to time. The only part of us that is confined and limited by time is our flesh. Our body has an expiration date, very much like the groceries you buy.

One might be reading this with the question, what does this have to do with identity? The answer is this; we are laying down a solid foundation on which to build. And that foundation is, God is the creator, and He is the same yesterday, today, and forever. God does not live in 'time' and therefore does not change. What was true in the beginning will be confirmed in the end. This is precisely why the Lord says He is the Alpha and the Omega, the beginning and the end, which leads to another truth. I am sure you have noticed that I use God, Lord, and Jesus in the same context. Before we dive into this truth, let us look at Colossians 1:15-18

15 He is the image of the invisible God, the firstborn over all creation. 16 For by Him all things were created that are in heaven and that are on earth, visible and invisible, whether thrones or dominions or principalities or powers. All things were created through Him and for Him. 17 And He is before all things, and in Him, all things consist. 18 And He is the head of the body, the church, who is the beginning, the firstborn from the dead, that in all things He may have the preeminence.

I hope you read it more than once before we unpack this powerful package of truth. Let's look deeper into the first verse, 'He is the image of the invisible God, the firstborn over all creation.' This passage very clearly says that you will never see God. God is invisible. The only way you will ever see God is through Jesus. Jesus is the image of God. Allow me to share an example. Imagine if I asked you to show me the wind. You might be prompted to say, "well don't you feel that breeze?" But I did not ask how the wind felt; I asked you to show me the wind. How can we show the wind? Do we open a jar and capture the wind? No matter how fast you close the lid, it will still be an empty-looking jar. Yes, there is air in it, but you cannot see it. How about we get a giant clear balloon and put air into it to the total capacity. Yes! We have captured air. So we quickly tie the end to hold all of the captured air and hold it up for all to see. But all we see is an empty balloon. So how can we ever see the wind?

Well, there is an interesting phenomenon called a tornado. This happens when warm, humid air collides with cold, dry air. The warm air travels up through the cold air and forms a funnel, and when that funnel grows and hits the ground, it becomes a tornado. It is a powerful force to be reckoned with. It is wind, compacted so tightly together and forced together into one place. Then and only then can one look at a tornado and say, that is wind. Once the wind is forced to gather at one place, it causes violence, and everything it touches will never be the same again. Tornados do not last long; they are here one minute and gone the next. But for the life of the tornado, the wind is visible.

Would you please follow my thought? Jesus is the image of the invisible God. let's look at the next verse in Colossians 1:16

16 For by Him all things were created that are in heaven and that are on earth, visible and invisible, whether thrones or dominions or principalities or powers. All things were created through Him and for Him.

When Jesus was born on this earth, the Bible says in 1 Timothy 3:16 that God was manifested in the flesh. It is a powerful statement because it states that God Himself, the invisible God, manifested in the flesh. It means that God became clear or evident to the eye or mind. So for the first time in the history of the world since the beginning. The invisible God was finally able to be seen, not only seen but seen in living tissue as a human.

Back to the analogy of the tornado I mentioned earlier, the air is everywhere. How can one see it? It can't be bottled to be made visible. Yet once the wind is concentrated in a tiny space, it becomes a visible tornado and is an unstoppable force. Jesus is that tornado made visible for a short time on this earth. And everything Jesus touched is never the same again. What a great thought. That all majesty, glory, and power of God is concentrated to one moment in one person. This person is Jesus Christ, the image of the invisible God. He touched down on this earth and destroyed everything He touched.

When I say the word destroy, I mean it completely. He put an end to the existence of (something) by damaging or attacking it. What did He destroy, you might ask? He came to destroy the works of the enemy. This truth is in 1 John 3:8

For this purpose, the Son of God was manifested, that He might destroy the works of the devil.

I am positive that those who have read that verse in the past, it rings differently now. There it is in black and white. The purpose for Jesus to be manifested on this earth was to destroy the works of the devil. Nothing would ever be the same again. Jesus is the image of the invisible God. Now let's look at the following scripture in the passage.

Colossians 1:17 *And He is before all things, and in Him, all things consist.*

What a great passage! No matter what exists, whether visible or invisible. Whether thrones, dominions, principalities, or powers. Jesus is ahead and above all things. No, and, ifs or buts. So let's quickly summarize. Number one, Jesus is the creator. Number two, Jesus is over everything. Jesus has complete dominion over everything. No matter how big anything is. All kingdoms, empires whether physical or spiritual, it does not matter. Jesus reigns supreme. I pray that you are getting a clear picture in your mind of a big, powerful God.

Finally, we are at the end of the passage.
Colossians 1:18 *And He is the head of the body, the*

church, who is the beginning, the firstborn from the dead, that in all things He may have the preeminence.

I might be getting ahead of myself in this book, but we have to talk about this scripture. It very clearly states that Jesus is the head of the body. That is very precise and understandable. What we don't seem to anchor within ourselves genuinely is that we indeed are His body. This is a big deal if you are a believer in Jesus. Earthly religion separates us from God. Religion exalts Him and leaves us as worms in the dirt. Do you realize how damaging this frame of thought is within the church? The moment we build our Christian belief system on this foundation, it creates a Christian life with no power or self-esteem.

No wonder the church is in its current state. Jesus did not come to smash us into the dirt, No! He came to make us a part of Him. So let's look at the definition of the last word of that verse, preeminence. It means superiority, noble or excellent qualities. Praise God! According to this passage, Jesus is superior and excellent, and we have the privilege of being His body. So by default, we also are those things through Christ. Do we fully realize what position this puts us in if we are in Christ? I am not talking about your home church or your denomination. I am talking about the true definition of the church. An assembly of people surrendered to Jesus. If Jesus is the head and we are the body, then that means all other things are beneath our feet since we are the feet of Jesus. God is the creator, and He is above everything. Nothing is on His level. So please keep this truth in mind as we dive deeper.

3

DOMINION AND IDENTITY

As we go into this next portion of the truth, let's all read what the Bible says about the creation of humanity.

Genesis 1:26-29

26 Then God said, "Let Us make man in Our image, according to Our likeness; let them have dominion over the fish of the sea, over the birds of the air, and over the cattle, over all the earth and over every creeping thing that creeps on the earth." 27 So God created man in His own image; in the image of God He created him; male and female He created them. 28 Then God blessed them, and God said to them, "Be fruitful and multiply; fill the earth and subdue it; have dominion over the fish of the sea, over the birds of the air, and over every living thing that moves on the earth." 29 And God said, "See, I have given you every herb that yields seed which is on the face of all the earth, and every tree whose fruit yields seed; to you, it shall be for food.

There is so much to unpack in reading this scripture that it would take a few books unto itself. So we are going to be specific to the subject of identity and authority. You can notice in reading verse 26 that humankind was created to have dominion. God has total dominion, and if He is creating a being to be in His image, they must also have dominion. Many may think that God made us in his image is only about anatomy. Yes, that is part of it, but not entirely. If we are to be made in the image of God, it is also His character, personality, and traits. I always use it as a reference, parents and a baby. Depending on the language of the parents, the baby will learn the same vocabulary. If the parents are joyful and happy, the baby will reflect that.

In the same way, when we were created, we were given the same attributes of God. We often believe we need to suppress our emotions, yet we have emotions because God has emotions. The problem with emotions is when they are not in line with the Lord, they can cause havoc in our lives. So by God giving them dominion, emotions, character, and attributes, they now have an identity. Someone to identify themselves with. In the beginning, Adam and Eve only had God to reflect on. They were not wicked because God was not wicked. They were not fearful because God was not fearful.

Let me hit the point even more profound by using an analogy. Many of us have either bought a car or purchased a home. When the purchase is made, you receive a piece of paper, a deed, or a pink slip. This piece of paper is a legal form stating that you are the rightful owner of said property. If anyone came into your home or broke into your car, that person has broken the law. But, what if you left the pink slip in the glove compartment of the vehicle. It would be easy for the thief to sign their name on the purchase line, and that person now legally owns the car. I know it would be a horrible thing to do, but the thief would show the pink slip in court, and it would be binding. So let's use this example in the beginning with Adam. The Lord dominates the universe, so He created Adam to dominate the earth. So in a sense, there was a legal, spiritual deed to the world. What an excellent opportunity for satan! The devil was envious and rebellious of God and wanted to dominate. If only he could take away the 'deed' from Adam, and this world would be his. Satan would become the god of this world.

Let us now read another portion of scripture in the book of Genesis 2:15-25

15 Then the Lord God took the man and put him in the garden of Eden to tend and keep it. 16 And the Lord God commanded the man, saying, "Of every tree of the garden you may freely eat; 17 but of the tree of the knowledge of good and evil you shall not eat, for in the day that you eat of it you shall surely die." 18 And the Lord God said, "It is not good that man should be alone; I will make him a helper comparable to him." 19 Out of the ground the Lord God formed every beast of the field and every bird of the air, and brought them to Adam to see what he would call them. And whatever Adam called each living creature, that was its name. 20 So Adam gave names to all cattle, to the birds of the air, and to every beast of the field. But for Adam there was not found a helper comparable to him. 21 And the Lord God caused a deep sleep to fall on Adam, and he slept; and He took one of his ribs, and closed up the flesh in its place. 22 Then the rib which the Lord God had taken from man He made into a woman, and He brought her to the man.

As we read the portion of scripture, it is clear that Adam was indeed given dominion. Yet, it came with a warning. God warned Adam, not Adam and Eve, but Adam alone. God warned him not to eat of the tree of knowledge of good and evil, or he would surely die. Also, notice that Adam was put in the garden to tend and keep it. He was given a job to do. It was Adam alone that named the animals and all living creatures. Once He named the animals, scripture tells us that Adam had no helper comparable to him. So the Lord caused Adam to fall into a deep sleep, and out of the rib of Adam, God created Eve. We know from scripture that God would meet with them daily to walk with them through the garden. There was open communication. Adam and Eve both learned from God, but Adam's responsibility was to teach his wife Eve all that the Lord had taught him. To summarize how glorious the creation of humanity is in the eyes of God, let's look at the following passage.

Psalms 8:5-6

5 *For You have made him a little lower than the angels, And You have crowned him with glory and honor.* 6 *You have made him to have dominion over the works of Your hands; You have put all things under his feet,*

When the Lord created us, we were crowned by God with glory and honor. We were never meant to be like an animal. Instead, we were given the ability to think, analyze, build and communicate. Once again, it is confirmed at the end of verse 6 that God has put all things under our feet. He put us in a position to dominate.

To set the stage for the next portion of the truth, we need to bullet point what we have learned so far.

- God alone is the creator.
- God created us in His image.
- God gave Adam dominion.
- God gave Adam a warning.
- God gave Adam a helper.
- God crowned humankind with glory and honor.
- God gave Adam and Eve an identity.

4

SHAME, CONDEMNATION, GUILT, AND FEAR

Adam and Eve are in the garden of Eden, with authority over all living things on the earth and reflecting the Lord Himself in their character. Then, suddenly we come across an interesting conversation between Eve and a serpent.

Genesis 3:1-12

Now the serpent was more cunning than any beast of the field which the Lord God had made. And he said to the woman, "Has God indeed said, 'You shall not eat of every tree of the garden'?"

2 *And the woman said to the serpent, "We may eat the fruit of the trees of the garden;*

3 but of the fruit of the tree which is in the midst of the garden, God has said, 'You shall not eat it, nor shall you touch it, lest you die.'"

4 Then the serpent said to the woman, "You will not surely die.

5 For God knows that in the day you eat of it your eyes will be opened, and you will be like God, knowing good and evil."

6 So when the woman saw that the tree was good for food, that it was pleasant to the eyes, and a tree desirable to make one wise, she took of its fruit and ate. She also gave to her husband with her, and he ate.

7 Then the eyes of both of them were opened, and they knew that they were naked; and they sewed fig leaves together and made themselves coverings.

8 And they heard the sound of the Lord God walking in the garden in the cool of the day, and Adam and his wife hid themselves from the presence of the Lord God among the trees of the garden.

9 Then the Lord God called to Adam and said to him, "Where are you?"

10 So he said, "I heard Your voice in the garden, and I was afraid because I was naked; and I hid myself."

11 And He said, "Who told you that you were naked? Have you eaten from the tree of which I commanded you that you should not eat?"

12 Then the man said, "The woman whom You gave to be with me, she gave me of the tree, and I ate."

Eve finds herself alone with a cunning creature. There is no scripture in the Bible that hints as to the whereabouts of Adam. A conversation begins with a question from the serpent. "Has God said you cannot eat from every tree in the garden?" This question was meant to derail and cause doubt. As a side note, always remember that the enemy does not use new tricks. His main objective was to cause doubt, and once doubt is planted, the rest fall like dominoes. Faith is such a huge part of following Jesus. Faith is the opposite of doubt. I am positive that Eve answered back with words that Adam taught her. It was the responsibility of Adam to share with Eve. We also need to understand that Eve was not wicked in her heart, nor was she gullible. She lived in an existence where there was no fear, wickedness, lies, or manipulation. She listens to the serpent, which is where the spiral began. Everything begins with who you listen to.

Romans 6:16

16 Do you not know that to whom you present yourselves slaves to obey, you are that one's slaves whom you obey, whether of sin leading to death, or of obedience leading to righteousness?

According to this scripture, when we obey something, we become a slave to it. The serpent knew what it was doing. There was a reason the serpent approached Eve and not Adam. Somehow it knew that if it could cause Eve to doubt and taste the fruit, that Adam would follow. The moment Eve tastes and realizes that she didn't instantly die, she gives it to Adam. At this point, Adam could have corrected her; he could have rebuked her. He did not; he also ate of the fruit. Adam directly disobedience to the Lord. Adam knew better, but he chose to obey his wife rather than God. And what happens when you obey? Yes, you become a slave to the one you obey. In that instant, they didn't die immediately, but death did come to them. They were eternal, and from that moment on, their bodies became mortal. What did happen instantly was a cloud of shame, guilt, condemnation, and fear. Shame because they knew right from wrong. Guilt because they had disobeyed the Lord. Condemnation because they have now become slaves to sin. Fear because what would the Lord do now after this scandalous event. They realized they were naked and ran into the bushes to cover their nakedness.

Once they covered their nakedness, they heard the Lord walking in the cool of the garden. Adam and Eve quickly hid in the trees. Notice what the Lord asks. "Where are you." It is important to pause here and talk about this question. Of course, one cannot hide from God behind a bush or tree. Even the scriptures say that if we go to the highest mountain, God is there. And if we make our bed in hell, He is there. So what did God mean with this question? I will share an example I often share when it comes to this subject. Many of us grew up with a loved one with many fond memories. As we grew up and grew apart, maybe that person became an alcoholic or a drug addict. Then at a reunion, you see the person with whom you were close. They are erratic, different, won't look you in the eyes when you speak to them. It confuses you because it feels as if they are another person. You want to grab onto their shoulders and shake them and say, "Where are you!" The person you once knew is no longer there. The life they had in their eyes has gone dim. The joy they had is now lost. I believe this is what the Lord meant when He asked Adam, "Where are you?" Where was the Adam He knew full of confidence? Where was the Adam that took on the character of God? The Adam God knew would have never hidden with shame. The confirmation is right there in the scripture; it says that Adam was afraid and hid. These are characteristics that Adam did not learn from God.

When Adam and Eve fell, a few things happened. Sin is like an infectious disease. Sin caused them to be stained. Sin was so infectious that it caused it to spread from Adam and Eve to their children and every child after that. There was nothing man could do to remedy himself. Regardless of what you do or do not do, you are infected. Many might say, "I live a good life, I don't cheat on my spouse, I don't steal." It doesn't matter; we are all infected by birth. Spiritually they died, and physically their bodies began dying because the wages of sin is death.

Romans 6:23 *For the wages of sin is death.*

This is why there is death for every human. Every single one of us begins to die from the first breath. When we get a job, we are working for a wage, and at the end of the week, we receive our compensation. We earned that wage for the work we did. Well, because of Adam, the wage or payment of our sin is death. This is why we die; this is why there is sickness, famine, war, violence, disease, and murder.

It left humankind unable to pay our way out of the wage we have coming, and everyone has a payday sooner or later. This is why the Apostle Paul cries out with these words in,

Romans 7:24 O *wretched man that I am! Who will deliver me from this body of death?*

Also, their identity was replaced with shame, guilt, condemnation, and fear. A righteous connection with God was broken from that moment. The deed or pink slip of the world was stolen from Adam, and Satan became the dominator of this world. Do you recall in the previous chapter how I explained that a pink slip being stolen and signed causes the thief to be the legal owner of the stolen vehicle? In a sense, this is what Satan did. It was the perfect plan for him—cause Eve to fall, which then caused Adam to fall. Sin came into the picture. Guilt, shame, condemnation, and fear are the symptoms of sin in Adam and Eve's hearts and every generation after. And just like that, all ownership is given to Satan, and he finally gets what he wants—total domination.

Would you please let this sink in? Adam and Eve lost their identity. Before the fall, they knew who they were. They knew who they belonged to. They had the deed of authority over the land, and they had a direct relationship with the Lord. This reminds me of a time when I was living in complete rebellion against God. I was in my mid-twenties and eating dinner at my parent's table. I was in a gang, selling drugs with a heart of violence. My mother, being a believer since I was five, looked directly at me. She didn't know exactly what I was doing, but she knew I was not the same boy she raised to love the Lord. She looked directly at me and said, "Where is the David I raised? Where is the one that loved to read the Bible as a child? Because this person in front of me is not the David, I know." Her words seared into my heart. I knew she was right, but I felt so far gone. I no longer reflected my mother and father, who raised me by example to love the Lord.

So we are left with the question, what is sin? We can describe it as an infection that has infected all of us. There was a popular show with zombies. Once a zombie bit a person, that person became infected. But as the episodes progressed, the characters soon learned a bitter truth. Even if they were not bitten, they were still infected. Every single one of them fought tooth and nail not to get bit, but it didn't matter; once dead, they too would become a zombie. As I write this book, we are amid a horrible sickness that has swept across the world. Scientists and doctors are scrambling for ways to stop infection. Many have taken a vaccine to help them stay safe; others wear masks, distance themselves from others and attempt to stay as healthy as possible. As bad as this sickness has affected the world, it is still nothing compared to the illness of sin. There is no vaccine, vitamin, or mask to hide from sin. We are all infected.

Romans 5:12 *Therefore, just as through one man sin entered the world, and death through sin, and thus death spread to all men because all sinned.*

This verse clearly states what I have written. One man's actions caused sin to enter the world, and because of that, death has spread to all men. Wow, a verse that holds no punches. Let's look at another verse.

Romans 5:14 *Nevertheless death reigned from Adam to Moses, even over those who had not sinned according to the likeness of the transgression of Adam, who is a type of Him who was to come.*

In this verse, sin equals death; even for those that did not disobey like Adam, death is still coming.

Therefore, I will share two more verses before we move on.

1 Corinthians 15:22a *For as in Adam all die*

Psalm 51:5 *Behold, I was brought forth in iniquity, and in sin, my mother conceived me.*

As we reach the end of this chapter, we cannot move on until we discuss broken communication. This has been a weapon the enemy has used time and time again. It is common knowledge that in a war, the first thing that must be done is to cut off your enemy's communications from their headquarters. This leaves your opponents scrambling to save themselves. It is strategic and divisive. This then causes chaos for those left behind enemy lines. When Adam fell, we left ourselves behind enemy lines to fend for ourselves with an enemy that utterly loathes us to the point of destruction. Humanity is left to our devices, our thoughts, and entirely left out in complete darkness. Now the god of this world has free reign to do as he pleases.

5

WHAT DID JESUS REALLY DO?

If this book had ended in the last chapter, it would have been a sorrowful story. Adam fell, and therefore we are all doomed. But it does not end there. We all know that Jesus came to die for our sins. See how easy that rolls off of our tongues? We have said it so many times that the heaviness that someone died for us gets lost. We are going to dig deeper and bring the weight back to the words of His death. This is the creator of all that exists we are speaking about. How can it be that He loved us so much? This is the part that atheists don't understand. If there is a God that created the universe, why would He even bother to save us? The atheist doesn't know that a follower of Jesus has the same question, "Why would the creator of all bother to save us?"

Yet this is precisely the question that draws us to Jesus. So let's look at this Bible verse.

1 Corinthians 15:45 *And so it is written, "the first man Adam became a living being." The last man Adam became a life-giving spirit.*

This verse confirms that Adam was the first man in the flesh. The part I want to point out is the last portion. It speaks of Jesus as the last Adam. So in the context of the passage, we know this is talking about the Lord Jesus. So why is it referring to Jesus as Adam? And what does this mean for us? To answer this, let's read another verse.

John 19:30 *So when Jesus had received the sour wine, He said, "It is finished!" And bowing His head, He gave up His spirit.*

Wow! What a powerful way to die on a cross. Many know these words of Jesus and assume that He is speaking only about suffering on the cross. It is understandable since He was suffering for so many hours. He was born in a manger, raised by Joseph and Mary. Taught the Scriptures as He grew up and became a teacher. He shared the gospel and about the Kingdom of God until He was arrested. But the words "It is finished" go back to thousands of years. There was something much more pressing for Jesus to 'finish.' He had an assignment to complete and reverse what Adam did. Let's revisit what Adam did in a bullet point.

- Adam lost humankind's authority on earth.
- Adam lost His Identity, now filled with shame, guilt, condemnation, and fear.
- By obeying Satan, Adam became a slave to sin.
- Adam brought death to all humans and creation.
- Adam infected himself and all after him with sin.
- Adam broke the line of communication being man and God.
- Adam ruined our status in right standing with God.
-

Let's look at another passage of Scripture.

Romans 5:12-14 (MSG) *You know the story of how*

Adam landed us in the dilemma we're in – first sin, then death. And no one exempt from either sin or death. That sin disturbed relations with God in everything and everyone, but the extent of the disturbance was not clear until God spelled it out in detail to Moses. So death, this huge abyss separating us from God, dominated the landscape from Adam to Moses. Even those who didn't sin precisely as Adam did by disobeying a specific command of God still had to experience this termination of life, this separation from God. But Adam, who got us into this, also points ahead to the One who will get us out of it.

This passage is incredible. According to the Word of God, Jesus came to completely undo, demolish and make right all that the first Adam did. Jesus came to do what the first Adam should have done. Read that list again because Jesus was the only one that could undo it. Every single one of the bullet points was smeared off the page. IT IS FINISHED! Wow, what a compelling, bold statement. I want to take some creative imagination for a moment. Knowing that the Word of God says that Satan is a created being means that only God can be at all places at all times. So during the crucifixion, where else would satan be in all of the earth at that time.

I ultimately believe that satan was right there, front and center, while Jesus was suffering. Maybe he was joyful watching the Lord suffer from each breath. Then out of nowhere, Jesus looks at the enemy in the face and declares victory. It is finished! I just undid all that you did to Adam. I just undid it, and there is nothing you can do to stop it. I take back the deed to this planet; I give back identity and destroy shame, guilt, condemnation, and fear. I break the chains of the slaves. I bring back life. My blood is the vaccine against sin. I replace communication by reconciling man to me. Brother and sister, this is the point of the book where you can just put it down and worship the Lord. Once Adam became enslaved to sin and infected all of us. It was impossible ever to get our authority, identity, and right standing back. God loved us so much and knew our predicament. Knowing that we were lost forever unless He came to undo it. Praise God, thank you, Jesus.

Remember the part that satan took the deed, even though he stole it; the fact was that he legally was the god and dominator of this world. This is precisely why you don't see demon possession in the old testament. Why would devils need to possess that which they already owned? But we will get into the details of that later on in the book. Jesus came to do what none of us could do for ourselves. This is why we never boast about what we did to gain our salvation because we did nothing. Jesus did it all.

I have loosely used 'deed' and 'pink slip' as an example of a legally binding contract to show proof of ownership. The Bible uses a specific legal term called a covenant. The definition of the word covenant is agreement. When a covenant is made, it is legally binding. When the Lord created Adam and gave him authority and dominion of the earth and every animal and creeping thing, it came with an agreement. The agreement was that Adam would not eat of the Tree of knowledge of Good and Evil. When Adam did eat the fruit of the tree, he voided all ownership, and the enemy was now in possession and control of the earth. With that in mind, let's rewind to the night before Jesus was crucified. I want you to notice something so powerful yet easy to pass by.

Luke 22:14-20 *When the hour had come, He sat down, and the twelve apostles with Him.*

15 *Then He said to them, "With fervent desire, I have desired to eat this Passover with you before I suffer;*

16 *for I say to you; I will no longer eat of it until it is fulfilled in the kingdom of God."*

17 *Then He took the cup, and gave thanks, and said, "Take this and divide it among yourselves;*

18 for I say to you, I will not drink of the fruit of the vine until the kingdom of God comes."

19 And He took bread, gave thanks and broke it, and gave it to them, saying, "This is My body which is given for you; do this in remembrance of Me."

20 Likewise, He also took the cup after supper, saying, "This cup is the new covenant in My blood, which is shed for you.

The context of this passage is each year, the Jewish people would celebrate and remember the Passover. It was in remembrance of the day the Lord freed them from the grip of Egypt. They have been celebrating the yearly Passover for generations. The fact that Jesus was celebrating the Passover on the night before He was crucified shows how strategic the Lord is. On the day of the Passover, a perfect lamb was slain and its blood placed on the doorpost of the home. This was a promise and covenant to the Hebrews that if He saw the blood on the doorpost, He would Passover that home, and every firstborn would be saved.

So as the disciples gathered around Jesus on that unforgettable night. Jesus prayed and broke the bread, then He took the cup and passed it to them. As they were drinking the cup, Jesus said, "This is a new covenant in My blood." Do you see what happened there? This is huge! When a new contract is written out, it automatically voids the contract before it. This is monumental because only God can re-write the contract. Everything the enemy stole from mankind was about to be given back. The deed the enemy held was about to be legally voided and nulled. I genuinely believe that the devil shook to his core and wanted to expedite the murder of Jesus. Not realizing this was the plan of Jesus all along. This is why Jesus says,

John 10:18 *No one takes it from Me, but I lay it down of Myself. I have power to lay it down, and I have power to take it again. This command I have received from My Father."*

So how does salvation work? If Jesus took back authority, how does that fix our infection of sin? These are good questions worth answering in detail. Only a sinless man could cure the sin infection, yet all men are born in sin. This is why the birth of Jesus through a virgin was the only way to reconcile the issue. He had to be a human, yet not be born from the seed of man. Remember, the seed carried the sin infection. Since Adam brought death to us all, Jesus came to bring life. This is why we need to unite ourselves to Jesus in His death and His life.

Romans 6:5-6 for *if we have been united together in the likeness of His death, certainly we also shall be in the likeness of his resurrection, 6 Knowing this, that our old man was crucified with Him, that the body of sin might be done away with, that we should no longer be slaves of sin.*

Jesus was the firstborn, the example for each of us. As he would die in the flesh, we need to die to our old self. This is the only way to activate the new covenant in our lives. How does one die to our old life? By giving our life and surrendering it to Jesus. Jesus did not come to fix you; He came to kill you. Jesus died on the cross so that your old man would be crucified with Him. According to the above Scripture, this is how we can be freed from sin. In the same way, the Hebrews were saved from slavery from Egypt; we are also saved by blood. Only this time, it is not a lamb who sheds its blood; it is Jesus. This is why Jesus is called the Lamb of God, who takes away the world's sins. The historical story of Egypt, the Hebrew slaves, and Moses was a shadow of the world, our slavery to sin and Jesus. So, according to the above Scripture, we are no longer slaves of sin once we crucify our old man. Praise God! Thank you, Jesus, for saving me from what I could not free myself.

6

JESUS TAKES IT ALL BACK

Colossians 1:19-20 *For it pleased the Father that in Him all the fullness should dwell, 20 and by Him to reconcile all things to Himself, by Him, whether things on earth or things in heaven, having made peace through the blood of His cross.*

This is a very loaded passage. Once Jesus rose from the dead, all the fullness of God would now dwell in Him. This is a compelling statement unto itself. There is a power shift from the invisible God to the visible Christ. All the essence of God, His attributes, glory, power and, sovereignty rested on Jesus once He was resurrected. This was incredible, unthinkable. He became the bridge for us to come back into righteous standing. To be in righteous standing is for all debt to be paid. It means that you are in right standing with God. Because of the sin of Adam, we could never be in right standing nor earn it. Satan knew this and considered us his slaves for eternity. But Jesus came to make all things new. Sin was now dealt with, and peace between God and man could happen. What Jesus did is truly beyond fully comprehending. What He did on the cross not only shook the earth but heaven as well. It was like hitting reset on your computer. All was made new.

Revelations 1:18 *I am He who lives, and was dead, and behold, I am alive forevermore. Amen, And I have the keys of Hades and of Death.*

So the moment Jesus resurrected from the dead, He defeated the most significant obstacle of all, Death. The Bible states,

1 Corinthians 15:55-57 O *death, where is thy sting?* O *grave, where is thy victory? 56 The sting of death is sin; and the strength of sin is the law. 57 But thanks be to God, which giveth us the victory through our Lord Jesus Christ.*

This had never been accomplished since the time of creation. No matter how righteous the prophets and priests were in life, Death still won. Every child, man, and woman faced this unstoppable evil entity. You might ask why I am speaking as if Death is a person? I say this because the Bible reads as if Death is a person. By Jesus rising from the dead, there was no victory for Death. Jesus rose from the grave, defeated death, and took away its keys. This is what Jesus meant when He said,

John 11:25-26 Jesus said to her, *"I am the resurrection and the life. He who believes in Me, though he may die, he shall live. 26 And whoever lives and believes in Me shall never die. Do you believe this?"*

This statement is a declaration of war against Death. It is a promise that those who believe in Jesus will never die. Death was a curse upon Adam; that curse has now been lifted and nailed to the cross of Jesus. Praise God! Salvation is only simple because He did all the work. Salvation is accessible and attainable only because Jesus did all the work.

When I say that Jesus defeated Death and now we will never die, please don't get it confused with our body dying. But, of course, our bodies die, our flesh. But we are not our flesh. That is not what determines who we are. Our flesh is a vessel—our true selves in our soul. Jesus died so that those who die in Him will never taste death. That is precisely why Jesus says that whoever believes in it shall never perish.

So now that we have established that Jesus defeated death, we need to get deeper. I hope you are ready. It begins with a simple question. Is salvation a finished work or a current work? Let me explain before we move forward by defining both.

Definition of finished work: This means that what Jesus did on the cross is complete. It truly is and was finished with nothing to be added to salvation. It bases our salvation on simply accepting that He died on the cross, paid the cost for our sin, and was resurrected. Most believe this way without genuinely grasping what this means for us today. This truth is a game-changer.

Definition of a current work: This is the opposite of a finished work. This would mean that each time a person accepts or surrenders their life to the Lord, salvation is given to the person asking. That even though Jesus died over two thousand years ago for our sins, He still is at work saving thousands as they repent. Why is this important? Because this belief is rooted in the belief that Jesus is constantly saving each person one by one.

Okay, it might be possible that the two definitions still left your curiosity unanswered. I believe that through Scripture that what Jesus did on the cross is a finished work. There is nothing more He has to add to save us. It is finished! Meaning He died once and for all humanity. Those who lived before Him and those who will live after Him can all be saved. Let's look at 1 Timothy 2:3-4

3 For this is good and acceptable in the sight of God our Savior, 4 who desires all men to be saved and to come to the knowledge of the truth.

This passage is powerful because it lets us know the will of God. Jesus desires ALL men to be saved. This means there is no guesswork on who the Lord longs to be saved. Every single person we come across, the Lord wants for them to be saved. There is no need to pray before speaking to each person to ask God if this person needs to be saved. So, according to the Word of God, there are no and, ifs, or buts for the call of salvation. I do not believe that anyone can argue with this truth, which leads to my next point.

Because I know that God desires all men to be saved, this truth helps me in ministry. And because it's a finished work, this further helps me. This means that I can share, teach and preach over and over and over to the same person. So I cannot give up. I know that God desires for each person to be saved. But this does not always happen, does it? Does every person I share the gospel with get saved? No, of course not. But this does not take away from the desire that the Lord wants them to be saved. So I am freed to continue preaching salvation with this truth whether only one in the crowd surrenders to the Lord or a multitude.

In summary, this point is very important in light of the next chapter. So let me clearly say it, Jesus desires all to be saved, yet not all get saved. This does not change that we believers need to stand in faith and believe that Jesus pays for every person we come across.

7

THE WHIPPING POST

This chapter is crucial in identity teaching. It is a subject either ignored or glossed over. Every good Bible scholar or teacher will tell you that every single thing Jesus did during His life was essential. Jesus knew He had a short time and was very strategic in His words and actions. In the previous chapter, we see that it was pivotal that He died on the cross. This was the only way to undo what Adam did. Blood had to be shed for a new covenant. This single act was necessary, and there is no Christian denomination in the world that would deny that. So we sing, preach, teach about the cross and Jesus dying on it all year long. This single act was the only way for sins to be forgiven. This leads me to this next point.

If the crucifixion of Jesus was all we needed for

the forgiveness of sins, then why the whipping post? Remember, everything Jesus did was necessary. If He had never been whipped, we would have still been forgiven of our sins. It would not have changed anything about the good news of the Kingdom of God. He would have still resurrected in power, and we all would still be given the opportunity of salvation. So I'll ask again? Why the whipping post? There must be a reason He was tortured in such a horrible way. It's too easy to brush it off and say, well, it wasn't up to Jesus. Pontius Pilate ordered it, and the Roman soldiers did it. No, it's not that easy. We must remember that all of it was the plan of Jesus. He said that He could have called down legions of angels.

Matthew 26:52-54 *But Jesus said to him, "Put your sword in its place, for all who take the sword will perish by the sword. 53 Or do you think that I cannot now pray to My Father, and He will provide Me with more than twelve legions of angels? 54 How then could the Scriptures be fulfilled, that it must happen thus?"*

Jesus also said that nobody could take His life.

John 10:18 *No one takes it from Me, but I lay it down of Myself. I have power to lay it down, and I have power to take it again. This command I have received from My Father."*

The direction and narrative of His life and death were always in the control of Jesus. So again, I ask, why the whipping post? To begin to dive into this subject, let's go to the Old Testament book of Isaiah 53:5.

But He was wounded for our transgressions,
He was bruised for our iniquities;
The chastisement for our peace was upon Him,
And by His stripes, we are healed.

The entire chapter of Isaiah 53 is the most descriptive prophecy of the coming Messiah, Jesus Christ. I want to focus on verse five, At the end of the verse. It says by His stripes; we are healed. The Hebrew word used for Healed is 'raw'faw' (rapha). This word is a compound word that broadly means the wholesomeness of health. So the prophet Isaiah used the word 'rapha.' This verse directly says that by the stripes or whipping that the Messiah would take, it would be for the wholesomeness of our health. I have often heard this verse saying that we would be forever healed of earthly illness in heaven. But the cross has already sealed that. Jesus dying on the cross is how we would be healed forever. Some have said that this is not talking about physical healing but healed from sin. Again, that is what dying on the cross does for us. If Jesus had not been whipped, we would still have our salvation. So why the whipping post? This word 'rapha' is used again in Exodus 15:26

And said, "If you diligently heed the voice of the Lord your God and do what is right in His sight, give ear to His commandments and keep all His statutes, I will put none of the diseases on you which I have brought on the Egyptians. For I am the Lord who heals you."

In this verse, the Lord commands that if the people listen to His commandments and obey His statutes, the diseases on the Egyptians won't come upon them because He is the Lord who heals you. Or, in other words, gives wholesomeness of health.

Another small word in Isaiah 53:5 is the word 'are.' And by His stripes, we ARE healed. Notice it is in the past tense. As if it's already a finished work. So whatever happened on the whipping post is past tense; it is complete, finished. Healing is not something that we earn; it is already paid for. Isn't this the same with the crucifixion? We can receive salvation because the debt has already been paid in full. If Jesus was whipped for our healing, then this too has been paid in full. This is why Jesus said, "It is finished." Jesus undid all that Adam caused. He made way for man to be in right standing with God. He defeated death once and for all. He reconciled the world and made a bridge back to God. And He paid for sickness on the whipping post and has given us healing in the past tense.

What am I saying? I am saying that in the same way Jesus died for every single human on this earth, He also suffered at the whipping post for every single human on this earth. Does this mean we are all saved? No, millions have died and will never enter His gates. In the same way, not all will be healed in this fallen world. Both of these require faith. But if the option is there for everyone to receive salvation, then the option is also there for everyone to receive healing. It is a gift. Salvation is a gift, and so is healing.

What if I told you that the healing is not even about you? What if we look at the entire subject wrong. Perspective is everything. So let's summarize before we go on. Jesus dying on the cross and paying our debt means that every person the enemy causes to go to hell was stolen goods. Because Jesus paid the debt. And if Jesus paid for our healing, then every sick and diseased person is also stolen goods from Him. Because Jesus already paid the debt. So in actuality, us being ill or going to hell is not even about us. It is about satan taking from Jesus what rightfully belongs to the Lord. If you love Jesus, this should bother you. If Jesus is your King, then you should do everything possible for Jesus to get what belongs to Him.

I want to use an illustration of the Olympics. Athletes from all around the world gather to compete while the world watches. The athletes train for many years through different climates and strenuous work—all for the gold medal. The winner will stand with their back straight and their head held high. The winner is announced, the crowd cheers as the medal is put around their neck. The winning athlete deserves the cheers; they worked so hard and persevered. They earned the reward. Nobody could argue that the winning athlete deserved the gold medal.

In the same way, Jesus won the competition. He paid every debt of every human of the past, present, and future. Each of us is a medal to be put around His neck. A medal He deserves. So each person we lead to Christ is a medal around His neck, each healing is a medal around His neck. Jesus Christ deserves His reward. The salvation, the healings, the deliverance of demons is not about you. It was never about you or me. It's always been about Jesus getting the reward He paid for. I am hoping this changes your perspective on salvation, healing, and deliverance. These rewards are not yours or mine. These rewards are not about us building a more extensive ministry or platform. These rewards are not ours to flaunt on Youtube or Facebook. These rewards are for the one that paid the cost for them. Jesus deserves His reward!

I will drive this home with this passage.

Luke 15:7 *I say to you that likewise there will be more joy in heaven over one sinner who repents than over ninety-nine just persons who need no repentance.*

I often thought of this verse as all of heaven rejoicing when I surrendered my life to the Lord. But I failed to realize that I wasn't the winner; I was the medal. When the athlete wins the gold medal and the crowd cheers, the cheers are not for the medal. The cheers are for the person that shed sweat, blood, and tears to win. In the same way, all of heaven rejoices when a sinner repents because Jesus receives His deserved reward. How beautiful a thought that all heaven praises the King of Kings for receiving what He paid for. And how beautiful the thought that in the same way, the athlete looks at the medal, the Lord looks at us, His reward. Something He cherished and suffered so much to gain. Thank you, Jesus, for all You did.

8

ARMIES OF ANGELS

We are going to now dive into what happened in heaven during the time of humanity on earth. I have never heard it spoken of as it overlaps our timeline here on earth. So before we do this in the next chapter, we first have to lay a foundation of Biblical truth. That way, we can all come from the same understanding of context. Let's begin with heavenly beings called angels. In the Bible, there are close to three hundred mentions of angels. That is enough times to let us know that they are real, they play an essential role, and we need to learn a bit about them. So I'll begin with this interesting scripture.

Psalm 46:7 *The Lord of hosts is with us; The God of Jacob is our refuge. Selah*

Reading this verse alone will make sense to pass it by, yet this reference to the Lord as the Lord of hosts is mentioned 261 times in the Old Testament. So we need to give pause and precisely define why God is given this title so many times.

Definition: Lord (God) of hosts, God as Lord over earthly or heavenly armies.

So, according to this definition, God is a leader, a general of an army. This means that the angels in heaven were created to be soldiers. They are an army with different roles. In the same way, our military forces have different roles with each soldier. Some are fighters on the front line; others are in communications etc., etc. Also, in an army, there is a ranking structure. Some have more authority than others. When one joins the military, it is no longer about themselves; it is about the whole. They are to separate themselves from civilian life and only focus on the mission at hand. So it is not hard to imagine that angels were created to follow orders, file in military rank, and obey their leaders. They do not have free will in the same way humans do. They are eternal creatures that follow the orders of God, the Lord of the armies.

Maybe I am sharing something with you that you've already known or figured out. But let's go deeper. This truth then means that fallen angels are also soldiers with different roles. They are military-minded and focus on the mission at hand. Yes, they are fallen and now follow a different leader other than God, yet they are still soldiers. How could I possibly know this? Because this is what they were created to be. That means that fallen angels or demons have a rank and leaders above them. I explain this because many believe demons are not organized or floating around chaotically like the ghosts in the movie Ghostbusters. As if they are running around screaming, causing havoc, and laughing as we humans sin. Maybe we'd like to believe this because it makes demons less of a threat. Almost as if they are crazed animals like the movie Gremlins. No, my friend, this is not true. They are eternal soldiers that are focused on their mission and do not rest or sleep. So let's look at another verse.

Colossians 1:15-16 *He is the image of the invisible God, the firstborn over all creation. 16 For by him all things were created that are in heaven and that are on earth, visible and invisible, whether thrones or dominions or principalities or powers. All things were created through Him and for Him.*

This verse mentions thrones, dominions, principalities, or powers. This gives us a hint that there are spiritually wicked thrones, dominions, principalities, and powers. Of course, these can be physical places. Nations and kingdoms. But the verse says explicitly visible and invisible. This means that those places are also in existence in the spiritual realm. Thrones, dominions, and powers are pretty self-explanatory. What jumps out is the word principalities. This word is not often used. Let's look at the definition.

Principalities – A state ruled by a prince.

This again teaches us that fallen angels, otherwise known as demons, have a structure and rank. Some fallen angels have a higher rank within their wicked armies, even to the point of a prince over a principality. So demonic forces have territories, with a prince overseeing its jurisdiction with lower-ranked demons within that principality. So let's look at another verse.

Ephesians 6:11-12 *Put on the whole armor of God, that you may be able to stand against the wiles of the devil. 12 For we do not wrestle against flesh and blood, but against principalities, against powers, against the rulers of the darkness of this age, against spiritual hosts of wickedness in the heavenly places.*

This verse hits the nail on what I am writing about. First of all, it implies that believers are also soldiers. Only soldiers need to wear armor. But the armor is spiritual, not physical. We know this because it states that we are not fighting against other men if we continue reading. We do not wrestle against flesh and blood. Then it expresses what we are fighting. We are fighting against principalities. There are demon princes that oversee neighborhoods, cities, states, and nations. They oversee regions. We fight against powers and rulers of the darkness. Against spiritual hosts, or armies or wickedness. This passage gives a Biblical anchor for all I have taught thus far. The fact that fallen angels are wicked does not take away the fact that they are soldiers. I live in northern California. When I drive from city to city, It is clear to see the difference in principalities from one and another. Stockton feels different than Oakland, and San Jose feels different than San Francisco. Each is a principality with a different prince. In the same way, states feel different; nations feel different.

Now that we established the fact that angels are

soldiers. Let's go to our Bible and see what types of angelic beings the Bible talks about.

CHERUBIM

Genesis 3:24 *So He drove out the man; and He placed cherubim at the east of the garden of Eden, and a flaming sword which turned every way, to guard the way to the tree of life.*

Exodus 25:18-20 *And you shall make two cherubim of gold; of hammered work you shall make them at the two ends of the mercy seat. 19 Make one cherub at one end, and the other cherub at the other end; you shall make the cherubim at the two ends of it of one piece with the mercy seat. 20 And the cherubim shall stretch out their wings above, covering the mercy seat with their wings, and they shall face one another; the faces of the cherubim shall be toward the mercy seat.*

By reading this verse, we can see that Cherubim are guards, and they carry swords. We can also see that these are winged angels. I make this a point because the word angel is generalized as if there is only one type of angelic being in heaven. The Bible never states that every angel has wings. So when the Lord created these angelic beings, he created them equipped for whatever purpose they were created.

Also, a good thing to note is it seems only higher-ranking angelic beings have wings. This is important to note for further study into fallen angels of higher ranking.

SERAPHIM

Isaiah 6:1-7 *In the year that King Uzziah died, I saw the Lord sitting on a throne, high and lifted up, and the train of His robe filled the temple. 2 Above it stood seraphim; each one had six wings: with two he covered his face, with two he covered his feet, and with two he flew. 3 And one cried to another and said: "Holy, holy, holy is the Lord of hosts; The whole earth is full of His glory!" 4 And the posts of the door were shaken by the voice of him who cried out, and the house was filled with smoke. 5 So I said: "Woe is me, for I am undone! Because I am a man of unclean lips, and I dwell in the midst of a people of unclean lips; for my eyes have seen the King, The Lord of hosts." 6 Then one of the seraphim flew to me, having in his hand a live coal which he had taken with the tongs from the altar. 7 And he touched my mouth with it, and said: "Behold, this has touched your lips; Your iniquity is taken away, And your sin purged."*

Revelation 4:8 *The four living creatures, each having six wings, were full of eyes around and within. And they do not rest day or night, saying: "Holy, holy, holy, Lord God Almighty, Who was and is and is to come!"*

Seraphim are only mentioned within the throne room of God. We never read about Seraphim doing anything else but constantly praising God. These creatures have six wings. What is amazing and testimony about the holiness and glory of God is that these creatures, having no sin, still cannot look upon the Lord. Their eyes are constantly covered as they cry to one another of the holiness of God. My point is not an exhaustive study on these creatures, but to show that God created these many types of angelic beings with different purposes, duties, and responsibilities.

ARCHANGELS

Daniel 10:13 *But the prince of the kingdom of Persia withstood me twenty-one days; and behold, Michael, one of the chief princes, came to help me, for I had been left alone there with the kings of Persia.*

Daniel 8:15-16 *Then it happened, when I, Daniel, had seen the vision and was seeking the meaning, that suddenly there stood before me one having the appearance of a man. 16 And I heard a man's voice between the banks of the Ulai, who called, and said, "Gabriel, make this man understand the vision."*

Luke 1:19 *And the angel answered and said to him, "I am Gabriel, who stands in the presence of God, and was sent to speak to you and bring you these glad tidings.*

Jude 9 *Yet Michael the archangel, in contending with the devil, when he disputed about the body of Moses, dared not bring against him a reviling accusation, but said, "The Lord rebuke you!"*

Archangels are most recognized. The angels Michael and Gabriel are mentioned repeatedly in the Scriptures. Not much is said about archangels, but we can summarize that they are highly ranked and continually dwell in the very throne room of God. We also know, because of Daniel 10:13, that Michael is one of the chief princes. This is an excellent indicator that archangels are ranked as princes, which again shows that not all angels are the same. In other words, Michael didn't climb up in the ranks; God created him for that exact position. Other than the Seraphim who are constantly worshipping God, the only other beings we see with continual access to the throne room of God are archangels. This is a big clue that the archangels are overseers over regions. These prince archangels are given principalities to watch over, but it seems Michael is one of the princes over other princes. This might seem trivial, but this is very key and important to understanding how fallen angels operate and think.

ANGELS

These subsequent few passages are a few instances where angels are mentioned. We can learn a few things about these beings by reading. First, we can see that angels do come into the throne room at times to worship. We also learn that the number of them is immense. In the Luke passage, we can read that they also gather to sing praises. In the 2 Kings account, we read that some angels are warring angels. With horses and chariots. In the passage in Genesis, Jacob saw a ladder with angels going up and down from heaven. This lets us know that angels travel back and forth from earth to heaven. Once again, this point is important as we dive deeper into the next portion of this chapter and the next. Finally, my last point is in the passage of Matthew 28, at the tomb of Jesus. An angel came from heaven and rolled back a stone that would have taken a group of men to move. So we know they have supernatural strength. Also, the very sight of them caused soldiers to be afraid. This is a reminder of the fear of Moses when he came down the mountain with his face glowing. Being in God's very presence caused his face to glow; it made the people afraid. He was asked to wear a veil over his head for many days. Yet this same angel that brought fear to the soldiers guarding the tomb was meek when addressing the women.

Revelation 7:11 *All the angels stood around the throne and the elders and the four living creatures, and fell on their faces before the throne and worshiped God,*

Revelation 5:11-12 *Then I looked, and I heard the voice of many angels around the throne, the living creatures, and the elders; and the number of them was ten thousand times ten thousand, and thousands of thousands, 12 saying with a loud voice:*

"Worthy is the Lamb who was slain
To receive power and riches and wisdom,
And strength and honor and glory and blessing!"

Luke 2:8-14 *Now there were in the same country shepherds living out in the fields, keeping watch over their flock by night. 9 And behold, an angel of the Lord stood before them, and the glory of the Lord shone around them, and they were greatly afraid. 10 Then the angel said to them, "Do not be afraid, for behold, I bring you good tidings of great joy which will be to all people.* 11 *For there is born to you this day in the city of David a Savior, who is Christ the Lord.* 12 *And this will be the sign to you: You will find a Babe wrapped in swaddling cloths, lying in a manger."* 13 *And suddenly there was with the angel a multitude of the heavenly host praising God and saying:* 14 *"Glory to God in the highest, And on earth peace, goodwill toward men!"*

2 Kings 6:17-20 *And Elisha prayed, and said, "Lord, I pray, open his eyes that he may see." Then the Lord opened the eyes of the young man, and he saw. And behold, the mountain was full of horses and chariots of fire all around Elisha.* 18 *So when the Syrians came down to him, Elisha prayed to the Lord, and said, "Strike this people, I pray, with blindness." And He struck them with blindness according to the word of Elisha.* 19 *Now Elisha said to them, "This is not the way, nor is this the city. Follow me, and I will bring you to the man whom you seek." But he led them to Samaria.* 20 *So it was, when they had come to Samaria, that Elisha said, "Lord, open the eyes of these men, that they may see." And the Lord opened their eyes, and they saw; and there they were, inside Samaria!*

Genesis 28:12 *Then he dreamed, and behold, a ladder was set up on the earth, and its top reached to heaven; and there the angels of God were ascending and descending on it.*

Matthews 28:2-5 *And behold, there was a great earthquake; for an angel of the Lord descended from heaven, and came and rolled back the stone from the door, and sat on it. 3 His countenance was like lightning, and his clothing as white as snow. 4 And the guards shook for fear of him, and became like dead men. 5 But the angel answered and said to the women, "Do not be afraid, for I know that you seek Jesus who was crucified.*

9

HEAVENLY ASSIGNMENTS

Now that we have learned about different types of angelic beings, I wanted to dive a bit into the subject of assignments. If angelic beings are part of an army, then they each have different responsibilities. So I want to use this chapter to highlight a few of those mentioned in Scripture. First, we need to be completely clear in our understanding of these angelic beings. Demons or fallen angels are exactly everything scripture speaks about all angelic beings, except they are no longer holy. They are still soldiers, they are still structured, and they still operate in ranks. What they were created to do, does not change. A fallen cherub is still a cherub; a fallen worship angel is still a worship angel; a prince angel is still a prince. The difference is who they are following now. This is crucial because a better understanding of angelic beings gives us a clear understanding of fallen angels. If we are to fight against these beings, we need to learn what Scripture says about them. So let's look at the first passage.

Holy One & Watchers

Daniel 4:13,17,23

13 *I saw in the visions of my head while on my bed, and there was a watcher, a holy one, coming down from heaven.*

17 *'This decision is by the decree of the watchers, And the sentence by the word of the holy ones, so that the living may know That the Most High rules in the kingdom of men, Gives it to whomever He will, And sets over it the lowest of men.'*

23 *"And in as much as the king saw a watcher, a holy one, coming down from heaven and saying, 'Chop down the tree and destroy it, but leave its stump and roots in the earth, bound with a band of iron and bronze in the tender grass of the field; let it be wet with the dew of heaven, and let him graze with the beasts of the field, till seven times pass over him';*

In reading these passages, we can see that some

angels have an assignment to be watchers. Very much like a soldier on a tower with binoculars, always looking about where trouble could be brewing. These angels are in communications. They relay back and forth to the throne room of God. These are not fighting angels; they do not have weapons. Or at least there is never any mention of a weapon with a messenger or watching angels. A very well-known angel is the angel Gabriel. His name means the mighty one of God. When the angel Gabriel is mentioned, it is never in a fighting or battle context. It is always to communicate a message. So let's look at three of these verses.

Daniel 9:21 *Yes, while I was speaking in prayer, the man Gabriel, whom I had seen in the vision at the beginning, being caused to fly swiftly, reached me about the time of the evening offering.*

Luke 1:19 *And the angel answered and said to him, "I am Gabriel, who stands in the presence of God, and was sent to speak to you and bring you these glad tidings.*

Luke 1:26 *Now in the sixth month the angel Gabriel was sent by God to a city of Galilee named Nazareth.*

By reading Luke 1:19, we can see that Gabriel holds

a very high rank in heaven with his claim to be the one who stands in the presence of God. This confirms the definition of his name, mighty one of God.

Warring Angels

According to Scripture, we know that some angels carry swords and shields. Most of us believe this, yet we never honestly think or believe these weapons do anything. What we must never assume is that these weapons are simply costuming or cosmetic. Remember, everything God creates is with a purpose. So this must mean that angels have weapons to fight in battle truly. So we have to get over the reality that even though our physical weapons cannot hurt a demon, it does not mean angelic weapons are also useless. I once heard it said like this. Even though demons and angels are eternal beings, they can still be hurt, maimed, and disfigured. I know this thought steps out of Scripture and into the testimony of believers in dealing with demons. But I still feel it necessary to mention. You can take this as supplemental information.

A well-known evangelist, author, and personal friend taught me the following. First, I give his information value because he was highly ranked in santeria (witchcraft mixed with catholicism) and has many experiences with demons. He teaches that demons will often show themselves and bring a fear upon people because of how they look. Not only are they grotesque and monstrous, but many are also maimed, hurt, limping, and disfigured. This is not by choice of the demon. They don't wish to be maimed, limping, or disfigured. Direct causes from previous battles with angels. They are eternal beings, so they cannot die. Instead, they continue living with injuries. Many times a demon will enter a person, and that person will suddenly be injured or hurt. They will go to doctors and specialists, and nothing can be found. I believe that what the person is often feeling is a manifestation of the demon's pain. Especially when the person is prayed for, the pain will shift in the body during the prayer. I'll give a biblical example.

Luke 13:10-13 *Now He was teaching in one of the synagogues on the Sabbath.* 11 *And behold, there was a woman who had a spirit of infirmity eighteen years, and was bent over and could in no way raise herself up.* 12 *But when Jesus saw her, He called her to Him and said to her, "Woman, you are loosed from your infirmity."* 13 *And He laid His hands on her, and immediately she was made straight, and glorified God.*

This is an interesting passage. In the context of what was happening, Jesus was healing many people. Yet for this woman, He didn't begin with a prayer of healing. This woman in pain was not only a cause of physical illness; the passage states that she had a spirit of infirmity. This demon had a back issue that manifested in her body. So before healing her, He first cast out that hunch-backed spirit. Then once the spirit was cast out, the Lord healed her back. This is a clue that a demon in pain will manifest that pain through the person many times. I am in no way saying this is the case every time. But I have personally dealt with these issues as a pastor when praying for healing in others.

Now back to the subject at hand. Warring angels. Let's look at another angel named Michael.

Daniel 10:13 *But the prince of the kingdom of Persia withstood me twenty-one days; and behold, Michael, one of the chief princes, came to help me, for I had been left alone there with the kings of Persia.*

Daniel 10:20-21 *Then he said, "Do you know why I have come to you? And now I must return to fight with the prince of Persia; and when I have gone forth, indeed the prince of Greece will come. 21 But I will tell you what is noted in the Scripture of Truth. (No one upholds me against these, except Michael your prince.*

In the context of this verse is the prophet, Daniel. He had prayed and fasted and had not received an answer. Each day he would wait for a response from the Lord. Finally, after twenty-one days, the angel Gabriel appeared. In verse 13, the angel explains that he was held back by the prince of the kingdom of Persia for twenty-one days. Let's talk about this part first before going into the second half of the verse. If Gabriel were speaking about a physical person, a prince of Persia, this would not make sense. How can a person hold back an angel for twenty-one days? This verse only makes sense in the context that a supernatural being was withholding him. A demonic high-ranking prince that did not want the message to be relayed back to Daniel. A prince, by default, oversees a principality. Also, note that this was a messenger angel, not a warring angel. We know this because he was sending a message back to Daniel. Then in the next half of the verse, the angel Gabriel explains how he finally got across. And behold, Michael, one of the chief princes, came to help me. Not only was Michael a warring angel, but he was a chief prince. A high-ranking angel of the

Lord. So it took a powerful holy prince to fight against the demonic prince of Persia.

In the second passage mentioned above, Daniel 10:20-21. This is also very interesting. This is the same angel speaking to Daniel. He says that for the angel to return to heaven, he has to fight the prince of Persia again and mentions that the demonic prince of Greece will be coming. So once again, Michael will have to help him get through.

I want to interject a thought here. There is a passage that Paul mentions in the New Testament speaking of a third heaven.

2 Corinthians 12:2-4 *I know a man in Christ who fourteen years ago—whether in the body I do not know, or whether out of the body I do not know, God knows—such a one was caught up to the third heaven. 3 And I know such a man—whether in the body or out of the body I do not know, God knows— 4 how he was caught up into Paradise and heard inexpressible words, which it is not lawful for a man to utter.*

Most scholars agree that Paul is being humble and speaking about himself in this passage. What stands out is that he describes the third heaven and defines that place as Paradise. Of course, one could never build an entire belief system from a faint mention, but we still need to talk about it. Many Scriptures describe the heavens as our atmosphere, our sky, and even our solar system. This can be based on truth according to Scripture. So if our atmosphere or realm is the first heaven, and the third heaven is Paradise or the place where God dwells. Is it that far of a stretch to say that the second heaven is a realm, a spiritual place, a chasm between both locations. A division between reality here on earth and heaven? If so, could this be the place that the angel Gabriel could not get across until the angel Michael helped? Could this be the spiritual realm that demonic beings dwell in? Could this be the reason Daniel's prayers took so long to get an answer? Lastly, can this be the place in which demonic princes oversee their principalities here on earth?

Let's look at Colossians 1:15-16

He is the image of the invisible God, the firstborn over all creation. 16 for by Him all things were created that are in heaven and that are on earth, visible and invisible, whether thrones or domininons or principalities or powers. All things were created through Him and for Him.

We used this verse at the beginning of this book, but we've learned so much since then. So here we are again, re-reading this critical passage. It mentions that there are thrones, dominions, principalities, and powers, whether visible or invisible. We know the visible powers. They are presidents, kings, princes, governors, mayors, judges, members of Congress, heads of state. These are visible offices of power that we know of. But the verse says visible and invisible. This, then, is a fact. There are invisible places of power. This coincides perfectly with the book of Daniel. The Angel Gabriel fought against the prince of Persia, a spiritual entity.

All of this leads us to read one more passage as we conclude this chapter.

Ephesians 6:11-12 *Put on the whole armor of God, that you may be able to stand against the wiles of the devil. 12 For we do not wrestle against flesh and blood, but against principalities, against powers, against the rulers of the darkness of this age, against the spiritual hosts of wickedness in the heavenly places.*

Everything we have spoken of regarding angels and demons can be hinged and anchored in this passage. Let's unpack the passage. We put on the whole armor of God. There is no reason for anyone to put on armor unless enlisted to fight in a war. So please get this engraved into your heart now. If you are a believer of Jesus, you have been drafted. We are targets the moment we move our allegiance from Satan to Jesus. Before Christ, by default, we were puppets for the enemy. We believed the lie and took on the identity of our kidnapper, which is satan. But now, in Christ, we must put on the armor of God. What is interesting is the following passage, we do not wrestle against flesh and blood. So obviously, this is not talking about physical armor, physical weapons, or tactical gear. What good would these things do if we are not fighting against flesh and blood? Our enemies are not people. No matter what nation, skin color, or belief. They are not the enemy. As the year's pass, this line gets more blurred by the moment. There are good God-fearing men and women of God that have missed the mark in this war. So what do we fight against, if not flesh and blood? The answer is in the rest of the verse. We wrestle against principalities, against powers, against the rulers of the darkness of this age, against the spiritual hosts of wickedness in the heavenly places.

This is who we should be fighting.

- Principalities – demonic forces with a prince overseeing regions
- Powers – demonic forces with the power to

influence physical powers

- Rulers of the darkness of this age – demonic rulers, these demons are high in the ranking system of satan. They are the generals, captains, and sergeants over nations, states, cities, and neighborhoods. Also, systems set in place such as politics, entertainment, witchcraft, gangs, cartels.
- Spiritual hosts, or spiritual armies in heavenly places.

The last point seems to lead to the invisible place in the heavens where these spiritual armies dwell. This makes sense when coupled with the situation the angel Gabriel had in reaching Daniel.

This chapter is not about fighting these forces but simply showing what they are and who they are. I will end it with this. If the Lord didn't feel we were equipped to fight this enemy, He wouldn't give us armor, to begin with.

10

THE WICKED ONES IN SOLITARY

I needed to take a few minutes on this subject before we went on to the next chapter. To summarize, we know that angels and demons are the same, except fallen angels are no longer holy and follow the Lord. It seems from Scripture that they continue in their rank and assignments, from the regular angel to the Cherubim and archangels in the throne room of God. Those that fell away continued to stay within their rank and authority over other fallen angels. So we get a glimpse of this truth in the book of Jude.

Jude 6 *And the angels who did not keep their proper domain, but left their own abode, He has reserved in everlasting chains under darkness for the judgment of the great day.*

Up to this point in the book, I have been referencing the NKJV Bible translation. But to drive the above verse home, I want to show how it reads in the Message Bible.

The Message Bible Jude 6 *Later, he destroyed those who defected. And you know the story of the angels who didn't stick to their post, abandoning it for other, darker missions. But they are now chained and jailed in a black hole until the great Judgment Day. Sodom and Gomorrah, which went to sexual rack and ruin along with the surrounding cities that acted just like them.*

Ok, let's unpack this verse. It speaks about angels that didn't stick to their post or their proper domain. This is a huge clue that can quickly be glossed over. This shows us that even though they are demonic fallen angels, they still have a post, rank, or position. So instead of staying in their post, they abandoned their position for darker missions. They were doing things that they were not allowed to do. Honestly, we don't exactly know what these fallen angels did, but it was so bad that the Lord put them in solitary. They have been chained since the beginning.

Many times we assume that satan is the worst of the worst. Maybe because we know he is the god of this world. But according to this Scripture, there are far worse demons than satan. They are so wicked and twisted that the Lord put them into solitary confinement in chains until the great Judgment Day. Wow! This is mind-blowing to think about. With so much murder, wars, death, disease, perversion, and hate already in this world, it is hard to imagine worse demons. Yet this must be true because we know that Satan walks to and fro on this earth freely. Here is another reference to these same wicked fallen angels.

2 Peter 2:4 *For if God did not spare the angels who sinned, but cast them down to hell and delivered them into chains of darkness, to be reserved for judgment*

(A footnote is there is no biblical reference that satan and his demons control hell, God created hell for satan and his angels; this is not a place they want to be at, much less call the shots there.)

So let's summarize before we get to the last part of this chapter.

- Angels are created to operate out of

structure, orders, and ranking

- Angels that did not stay to their rank have been cast in chains until Judgment Day
- Angels are designed to obey orders, whether fallen angels or holy angels.
-

I will use a part of my own life experience for the following example. I spent six years in federal prison. During my incarceration is when I surrendered my life to Jesus Christ. In prison is a place they call the hole, or solitary confinement. This is the place that is a prison within the prison. Prisons across the country are filled with people that cannot function in regular society. Many are too dangerous to be in our cities and neighborhoods. Prisons are built to protect society from criminals. But the prison has a prison within it for the worst of the worst. These inmates are so dangerous, so treacherous that they cannot be in the regular prison. The regular inmates need to be kept safe from those in solitary. Well, our earth is the prison yard for satan and his demons. They have been kicked out of heaven and are trapped on this earth and its atmosphere. But deep within, a place of utter darkness is the worst of the worst, locked in chains. I imagine that even the demons on this earth tremble at the thought of those most wicked demons. So please understand that there is no camaraderie or friendships within the ranks of devils. They have no compassion for one another and no brotherhood. Those would all be attributes of God, and they want nothing to do with God. Demons are so filled with hate, to the point they mistrust and hate each other. How can we know this? Because any good attribute of God is void in them. They are all sentenced to hell, and they know it. So let me give you a Biblical reference.

Matthew 8:28-32 *When He had come to the other side, to the country of the Gergesenes, there met Him, two demon-possessed men, coming out of the tombs, exceedingly fierce, so that no one could pass that way.* 29 *And suddenly they cried out, saying, "What have we to do with You, Jesus, You Son of God? Have You come here to torment us before the time?"* 30 *Now a good way off from them there was a herd of many swine feeding.* 31 *So the demons begged Him, saying, "If You cast us out, permit us to go away into the herd of swine."* 32 *And He said to them, "Go." So when they had come out, they went into the herd of swine. And suddenly the whole herd of swine ran violently down the steep place into the sea and perished in the water.*

In this passage, Jesus comes across two men full of

demons. They are so violent that nobody can pass by. Yet, the moment they see Jesus, they begin to cry out and beg. Listen to what they are saying. "Have you come here to torment us before our time?" This lets us know two things. First is they realize they are already sentenced. Second, they are afraid. Could it be that they feared being put into solitary with the most wicked demons? They knew this was a possibility and begged Jesus to allow them to go into the pigs instead. They would have done anything than to be sent into the abyss in chains of darkness.

My last point of this chapter is the Bible names one of these wicked ones. So let's read this passage.

Revelation 9:1-11 *Then the fifth angel sounded: And I saw a star fallen from heaven to the earth. To him was given the key to the bottomless pit. 2 And he opened the bottomless pit, and smoke arose out of the pit like the smoke of a great furnace. So the sun and the air were darkened because of the smoke of the pit. 3 Then out of the smoke locusts came upon the earth. And to them was given power, as the scorpions of the earth have power. 4 They were commanded not to harm the grass of the earth, or any green thing, or any tree, but only those men who do not have the seal of God on their foreheads. 5 And they were not given authority to kill them, but to torment them for five months. Their torment was like the torment of a scorpion when it strikes a man. 6 In those days men will seek death and will not find it; they will desire to die, and death will flee from them.*

7 The shape of the locusts was like horses prepared for battle. On their heads were crowns of something like gold, and their faces were like the faces of men. 8 They had hair like women's hair, and their teeth were like lions' teeth. 9 And they had breastplates like breastplates of iron, and the sound of their wings was like the sound of chariots with many horses running into battle. 10 They had tails like scorpions, and there were stings in their tails. Their power was to hurt men five months. 11 And they had as king over them the angel of the bottomless pit, whose name in Hebrew is Abaddon, but in Greek he has the name Apollyon.

As we read the end of the above passage, we see a name never used in the Bible. The Hebrew name Abaddon and in Greek Apollyon. This fallen archangel is the king of the bottomless pit. This demon has been in chains since the beginning. In English, his name translates to the Destroyer. Sometimes this confuses people because we know that Satan is the god of this world, so how can there be a worse demon. Being the strongest demon and the worst can be two completely different things.

Let me give an illustration. In gang life, the leader is usually not the most violent nor the most treacherous. The leader is the most manipulative influencer. And that leader will surround himself with the most violent. Satan is not a warring angel; he was also not a messenger angel. We have spoken of the different assignments given to each angelic being, but we have yet to dive into who exactly satan is and what kind of angel he was created to be. We can know for sure that he was and is a master manipulator to cause so many angels to defect from following and obeying the Lord. And satan continues to manipulate humans over the last few thousand years.

11

IDENTITY OF SATAN

Who is Satan, and why are we using so many pages and chapters talking about him and his fallen angels? Let me say it bluntly. The enemy wants to destroy you and me and will stop at nothing. They have studied us for centuries and know everything about our weaknesses, strengths, and how we function in different scenarios. Yet, we hardly take the time to learn anything about this enemy of ours. How can we ever begin to fight a battle against an unknown foe? These fallen angels do not sleep, do not eat, and do not take vacations. The Bible is full of truths about the character traits of these demons and how they operate. We need to use wisdom and take heed to whatever the Bible gives us. I'm positive we all agree that it must be important if something is written in the Bible. This leads to this chapter. The Bible does not describe satan exhaustively, but it gives us a lot more than most realize. There have been so many books, sermons, and studies on satan, and many times built on opinion, or even worse, on what demons say during deliverance. The latter is what worries me most. Not all, but many deliverance ministries have entire teachings on demons and casting them out that they have compiled by talking to demons. I find this strange because these same ministers will say that demons are liars. Jesus says this very clearly,

John 8:44 *You are of your father the devil, and the desires of your father you want to do. He was a murderer from the beginning and does not stand in the truth, because there is no truth in him. When he speaks a lie, he speaks from his own resources, for he is a liar and the father of it.*

So we must be careful in not building a belief system on demons by what demons say. The Word of God and the Holy Spirit within us will bring us to the truth.

So let's look into our first passage.

Ezekiel 28:11-19 *Moreover the word of the Lord came*

to me, saying, 12 "Son of man, take up a lamentation for the king of Tyre, and say to him, 'Thus says the Lord God: "You were the seal of perfection, Full of wisdom and perfect in beauty. 13 You were in Eden, the garden of God; Every precious stone was your covering: The sardius, topaz, and diamond, Beryl, onyx, and jasper, Sapphire, turquoise, and emerald with gold. The workmanship of your timbrels and pipes was prepared for you on the day you were created. 14 "You were the anointed cherub who covers; I established you; You were on the holy mountain of God; You walked back and forth in the midst of fiery stones. 15 You were perfect in your ways from the day you were created, Till iniquity was found in you. 16 "By the abundance of your trading You became filled with violence within, And you sinned; Therefore I cast you as a profane thing Out of the mountain of God; And I destroyed you, O covering cherub, From the midst of the fiery stones. 17 "Your heart was lifted up because of your beauty; You corrupted your wisdom for the sake of your splendor; I cast you to the ground, I laid you before kings, That they might gaze at you. 18 "You defiled your sanctuaries By the multitude of your iniquities, By the iniquity of your trading; Therefore I brought fire from your midst; It devoured you, And I turned you to ashes upon the earth In the sight of all who saw you. 19 All who knew you among the peoples are astonished at you; You have become a horror, And shall be no more forever."

At first glance, it seems to be that the context is talking about an earthly king. But if we continue reading past verse 11, we can see that the description cannot fit a human. Instead, it speaks about a created being that was perfect, full of wisdom, and beautiful. Then the hammer gets dropped on the following passage. "You were in Eden, the garden of God." We can only go as deep as Scripture, and we know there were two humans and a serpent in the garden of Eden. We also know that the two humans were made of flesh. Yet, this perfect beautiful being was not covered in flesh. It was created with precious stones and even had musical instruments in its body. Then it goes on to say that this created being was the anointed cherub. But, according to Scripture, we know that a cherub or cherubim are a high-ranking angel that dwells in the presence of God. In verse 14, it states the words' anointed cherub'. In other words, it was the chosen cherub—the selected out of all cherubs. So if we continue reading, we can see that this anointed being became corrupted; ego and pride came in because of how beautiful it was. Some scholars believe this is not a description of satan, but I genuinely believe it is. The Prophets often would write down what the Lord said, yet I wonder if even the Prophets truly understood with 100% accuracy the implications of what they were writing. Even in our modern times, we do things and say things that we do not fully understand. So let's write a bullet list of what we gather from this passage.

- This being was made with a seal of perfection
- This being was full of wisdom
- This being was perfect in beauty
- This being was in Eden, the garden of God
- This being was covered in precious stones
- This being had instruments built into its body
- This being was the chosen angelic being that covers
- God established this being
- This being was perfect until it fell into sin
- This being was filled with violence
- This being was cast out and destroyed
- This being was vain because of its beauty
- The Lord sent fire to devour the being
- The being became a horror

This is an excellent start to understanding who this being is and their character. Now let's read the passage of Isaiah 14:12-17

"How you are fallen from heaven, O Lucifer, son of the morning! How you are cut down to the ground, You who weakened the nations! 13 For you have said in your heart: 'I will ascend into heaven, I will exalt my throne above the stars of God; I will also sit on the mount of the congregation On the farthest sides of the north; 14 I will ascend above the heights of the clouds, I will be like the Most High.' 15 Yet you shall be brought down to Sheol, To the lowest depths of the Pit. 16 "Those who see you will gaze at you, And consider you, saying: 'Is this the man who made the earth tremble, Who shook kingdoms, 17 Who made the world as a wilderness And destroyed its cities, Who did not open the house of his prisoners?'

So let's see what we can learn from this passage. In the first verse, it mentions the name Lucifer. So it can be safe to say that this is the name satan had before he became satan. Verse thirteen through fourteen is interesting because it gives us a very proud and boastful being. If you notice, every sentence begins with the word, 'I.' Lucifer believed he should be exalted above God. Lucifer also thought he could be like God. What I find interesting are the last two verses. It says that those who gaze at him will know he's the one that brought havoc to the earth. He will be blamed for being the one to shake kingdoms.

So let's add a few bullet points to our list.

- Before the fall, his name was Lucifer.
- He was full of vanity and ego, believing he was like God
- He wanted to be exalted and worshipped.
- Others will look upon him and know who he is
-

Next, I will list a handful of other Bible verses; then, we will list a bullet point of characteristics of satan.

Matthew 12:24 *Now when the Pharisees heard it they said, "this fellow does not cast out demons except by Beelzebub, the ruler of the demons."*

2 Corinthians 4:4 *Whose minds the god of this age has blinded, who do not believe, lest the light of the gospel of the glory of Christ, who is the image of God, should shine on them.*

Matthew 4:1 *Then Jesus was led up by the Spirit into the wilderness to be tempted by the devil*

Ephesians 2:2 *In which you once walked according to the course of this world, according to the prince of the power of the air, the spirit who now works in the sons of disobedience*

1 Peter 5:8 *Be sober, be vigilant; because your adversary the devil walks about like a roaring lion, seeking whom he may devour.*

Genesis 3:1 *Now the serpent was more cunning than any beast of the field which the Lord God had made. And he said to the woman, "Has God indeed said, 'You shall not eat of every tree of the garden'?"*

Revelation 12:9 *So the great dragon was cast out, that serpent of old, called the Devil and Satan, who deceives the whole world; he was cast to the earth, and his angels were cast out with him.*

Matthew 4:3 *Now when the tempter came to Him, he said, "If You are the Son of God, command that these stones become bread."*

Ezekiel 28:14 *"You were anointed cherub who covers; I established you; You were on the holy mountain of God; You walked back and forth in the midst of fiery stones.*

2 Corinthians 6:15 *And what accord has Christ with Belial? Or what part has a believer with an unbeliever?*

Matthew 13:19 *When anyone hears the word of the kingdom, and does not understand it, then the wicked one comes and snatches away what was sown in his heart. This is he who received seed by the wayside.*

Okay, that was a whole list of verses that each

describe the character of satan. So let's write it in bullet points so we can better examine the traits.

- Beelzebub (prince of the demons) is the ruler of demons
- Satan is the god of his limited time, god of this earth
- He blinds those in darkness unless the Lord opens the eyes of the blind
- He is a tempter
- He is the prince of the power of the air
- He works in those that disobey God
- He is 'like a lion always seeking to destroy
- He causes you to question or doubt what the Lord has said
- He was the anointed (chosen one) angelic cherub
- He was on the holy mountain of God
- He is Belial, meaning without a master. Independent, self-sufficient
- He is wicked
- He snatches away what is sown in the heart.
-

As I said in the beginning, we must gather what we know about satan by what the Bible says. I hope it gave you a good summary in understanding who we are up against. This is not to make you afraid but to realize that our enemy intentionally seeks, kills, and destroys all we love, including ourselves. Knowing all we have learned in the previous chapter and this specific chapter will help piece together our understanding of the war in heaven. All of this is important in understanding our own identity in Christ. What war am I talking about? I am talking about the war of all wars.

12

WAR IN HEAVEN

For many of you, this book has stretched you in a way you never imagined. For others, it has given you hope you never had before. A few of you might be wondering why we are learning so much about angelic beings, fallen angels, and satan. What does this have to do with my identity? It has everything to do with our identity. The Bible says,

Ephesians 4:12-16 *for the equipping of the saints for the work of ministry, for the edifying of the body of Christ, 13 till we all come to the unity of the faith and of the knowledge of the Son of God, to a perfect man, to the measure of the stature of the fullness of Christ; 14 that we should no longer be children, tossed to and fro and carried about with every wind of doctrine, by the trickery of men, in the cunning craftiness of deceitful plotting, 15 but, speaking the truth in love, may grow up in all things into Him who is the head—Christ— 16 from whom the whole body, joined and knit together by what every joint supplies, according to the effective working by which every part does its share, causes growth of the body for the edifying of itself in love.*

I cannot teach identity to you by only giving you a portion of the truth. We need to understand who, what, how, and why. If we have to learn our identity, it raises the question of who took it from us? And if our identity was taken, then what happened? How was our identity taken, and why was it taken? In a war, there are many things at play. From the war rooms of national leaders and generals, all the way down to the trenches where two soldiers are fighting hand to hand combat, each fighting to survive one more day. One cannot honestly explain a war by ignoring how that war affects the leaders, soldiers, and civilians collectively. In reading Scripture, it is clear that we are called to be soldiers. So we are to fight a spiritual battle against an unseen enemy. But, according to the passage above, we must be equipped.

The only way to fully prepare a soldier is to explain the situation from beginning to end entirely. That way, we won't be tossed to and fro and carried about with every wind of doctrine. Most Christians are led to believe that the war in heaven ended at creation. That Satan and his demons rebelled against God and were cast out of heaven to earth. Then we've been taught that Adam and Eve were put into the garden of Eden, and that is where it all began. But, according to Scripture, I do not believe that the war ended at creation. So before I go further, let's read what the Bible says about the war in heaven.

Revelation 12:7-12 *And war broke out in heaven: Michael and his angels fought with the dragon; and the dragon and his angels fought, 8 but they did not prevail, nor was a place found for them in heaven any longer. 9 So the great dragon was cast out, that serpent of old, called the Devil and Satan, who deceives the whole world; he was cast to the earth, and his angels were cast out with him. 10 Then I heard a loud voice saying in heaven, "Now salvation, and strength, and the kingdom of our God, and the power of His Christ have come, for the accuser of our brethren, who accused them before our God day and night, has been cast down. 11 And they overcame him by the blood of the Lamb and by the word of their testimony, and they did not love their lives to the death. 12 Therefore rejoice, O heavens, and you who dwell in them! Woe to the inhabitants of the earth and the sea! For the devil has come down to you, having great wrath, because he knows that he has a short time."*

At this point, I believe it best to break this passage down verse by verse. By listing it in bullet form, it can be easier to digest. Let's begin.

- Verse 7 *And war broke out in heaven: Michael and his angels fought with the dragon, and the dragon and his angels fought.* This begins by simply noting that a war broke out in heaven. This is a fact that is Biblically sound. It did not mention when this war happened, but we know there was a war. Once again, we see the angel Michael mentioned again. We know that Michael is a warring angel and is a leader of other warring angels. Michael is the same angel that helped the angel Gabriel in the book of Daniel. In this passage, we also know who fought in this war. It was Michael and his angels against the dragon and his angels. A battle between good and evil, holy and wicked.

- Verse 8 *but they did not prevail, nor was a*

place found for them in heaven any longer. This verse lets us know that the dragon and his angels did not win. This allows us to understand that the battle in heaven is over; it is done. What did this mean for the losing side? It meant that they were kicked out of heaven. There was no place for them in heaven any longer. Both sides resided in the same area, which meant this was a civil war.

- Verse 9 *So the great dragon was cast out, that serpent of old, called the Devil and Satan, who deceives the whole world; he was cast to the earth, and his angels were cast out with him.* This is where it gets interesting. We begin to get a focus on a timeline of when this war happened. The verse says that the great dragon was cast out, then it calls the dragon the serpent of old. I find it interesting that the serpent is mentioned in the past tense. At the time of the war and casting out, it spoke of an earlier time that the dragon was indeed the serpent. All that have read the Bible know that the serpent it is speaking of is the serpent in the garden of Eden. Another significant clue is that satan had already been deceiving the world. How can he be deceiving the world if this war ended at creation? This only makes sense in the context that the fight happened at a later time. After man had already been on earth, to be deceived by satan. Also, once again, we see that Satan and his fallen angels were cast down to the earth. They were kicked out of heaven, with no heavenly access anymore. This is where we need to pause. We know from the book of Job and the book of Zechariah that satan still had access into the throne room.

•

Job 1:6-7 *Now there was a day when the sons of God came to present themselves before the Lord, and Satan also came among them. 7 And the Lord said to Satan, "From where do you come?" So, Satan answered the Lord and said, "From going to and fro on the earth, and from walking back and forth on it."*

Zechariah 3:1-2 *Then he showed me Joshua the high priest standing before the Angel of the Lord, and Satan standing at his right hand to oppose him. 2 And the Lord said to Satan, "The Lord rebuke you, Satan! The Lord who has chosen Jerusalem rebuke you! Is this not a brand plucked from the fire?*

This comes to the reality that the war could NOT have happened before creation. By satans own admission to God, he was back and forth on the earth accusing mankind.

- Verse 10 *Then I heard a loud voice saying in heaven, "Now salvation, and strength, and the kingdom of our God, and the power of His Christ have come, for the accuser of our brethren, who accused them before our God day and night, has been cast down.* This verse is packed full of vital knowledge in helping us unpack this passage. It states that the moment satan and his demons were cast out, now salvation was available, as well as the Kingdom of God. Notice this is the third time in this passage that Satan being cast out of heaven is mentioned. So the question needs to be asked. When did salvation become available? I will answer, salvation was made available at the death, burial, and resurrection of Jesus Christ. So this means that salvation was not possible until satan was cast down and kicked out of heaven. We also learn that he was called the accuser. This again leads us to the fact that satan still had access up to the point of Jesus dying on the cross. This is why he was able to continue to accuse the brethren day and night. This is a huge deal. I will summarize it all up at the end of these bullet points.

- Verse 11 *And they overcame him by the blood of the Lamb and by the word of their testimony, and they did not love their lives to the death.* This is the jaw-dropper. It confirms that Michael and his angels could not win this battle. It was a back and forth, constant fight. What finally finished the war was none other than the blood of Jesus. So the war could not have happened at creation.

- Verse 12 *Therefore rejoice, O heavens, and you who dwell in them! Woe to the inhabitants of the earth and the sea! For the devil has come down to you, having great wrath, because he knows that he has a short time."* This verse

> sums it all up. There is colossal rejoicing in heaven. They are rejoicing because Satan is no longer allowed into heaven. Jesus dying on the cross was the final blow to the enemy. The second part of the verse is a warning to us here on earth. It says that satan is coming down to us with great wrath, knowing he has a short time. This final sentence sums up the truth that he was not cast out of heaven at creation. He was thrown out of heaven at the resurrection of Jesus Christ, and because of that, will now come against the church.

Let us take a deep breath now. So much has to be summarized and repeated. First, we know there was a war. What we do not know is how long this war lasted. It could be that the war lasted from creation until the cross of Jesus. We know that satan rebelled in the beginning. How do we know this? Because he was the serpent of old, that caused Adam and Eve to fall. We also know that during the entire time between creation and the cross, satan accused mankind day and night. He had complete immunity to walk back and forth from earth and heaven. We also know that satan took over the world by taking all authority away from Adam during this time. During a war, each side has a headquarters. Satan made our planet his headquarters and has used the authority he took from Adam to become the god of this world. He has set up thrones and principalities. He has set high-ranking angels over regions with armies of demons under each prince. With the fall of Adam, this became a kingdom of darkness.

Once a kingdom is set up, it comes with rules. Those rules apply to those citizens of that kingdom. This is why Adam had to fall. Once mankind fell and was infected with sin, they became prisoners of this kingdom of darkness. That meant that all rules within the realm of darkness apply to its citizens. It also meant that satan became his own ambassador. When he traveled outside of his kingdom, he only lived according to his rules. He could travel to heaven as an ambassador of his kingdom with complete amnesty. The regulations of heaven did not apply to him because he was not a resident there. One would think that this would be okay with God. He and satan had their separate kingdoms, so leave it at that. There is a big problem, though; humans were made in the image of God. We are his most incredible creation. We were cheated out of our authority and dominion here on earth. God is a God of justice; this is beside the fact that God loves us.

God did not create this beautiful planet for satan to destroy; it was designed for us to enjoy. Satan's passport to go back and forth from heaven to earth had to be revoked. So a war went on for possibly centuries between Satan and God. So even though we don't know how long this war lasted, we know Jesus ended it. By the shedding of His precious blood.

The fact that Satan was kicked out of heaven. Thrown down to this earth. He can no longer enter into heaven, bound to our atmosphere and planet. For this reason, satan seeks to destroy us and kill us. We are a daily reminder of God. We are made in the very image of God. We are given hope where he no longer has hope. We are given mercy, where he has no mercy. And most of all, Jesus took the deed back from satan and has given it to the church. This is why we now have a fighting chance against satan and his demons. The rightful ownership has been given back to those that believe in Jesus. This means that any living thing on this earth is now under the dominion of those in Christ. Demons must submit to those that hold this authority. So the war has been moved from a war in heaven to a war on earth. The fight is now ours, for we do not fight against flesh and blood, but against principalities in high places.

There is one last point before we end this chapter.

Throughout these chapters, we have stated that angels were created with specific ranks and responsibilities. We know Michael is the prince of the warring angels. We know Gabriel is the messenger angel. There was a job opening left in heaven when Satan rebelled. Lucifer was a cherubim being that hovered over the throne of God. He was the most beautiful and had instruments built into his body. This could be for no other reason than to use those instruments to worship God. Some have even said that it is possible that Lucifer led worship with the four creatures that have six wings. If this is true, could it be that the job was left vacant for true worshippers who would worship God in spirit and truth? I don't believe it's a stretch to say that the church has been given this position, which further infuriates satan—what a beautiful thought—for us, born in sin, to be made righteous and allowed a place in heaven to worship God.

13

THE KINGDOM OF GOD

So much has been shared up to this point. For me, this part is the most exciting. It is that piece of the puzzle that, once put in place, brings clarity. Jesus often talked about the Kingdom of God throughout His short ministry. It was a phrase He often used, sometimes calling it the Kingdom of Heaven. In the book of Matthew alone, it mentions the Kingdom of Heaven 32 times. Also, depending on which translation you are reading, the New Testament says it over 100 times.

Interestingly, in our modern times, most teachings or sermons are not about the Kingdom of God. Why is that? I think this is a question that needs to be answered, or at the very least, examined. If we are not taught about the Kingdom of God, then identity teaching falls apart. So how can one boldly walk in their identity if they do not know where they belong? The Bible says we are not of this world. So what world are we from?

I would like first to establish a few truths so we can stay in context. At this point in the book, we know that there is a heaven. It is the dwelling place of the Lord, and He is God and Lord over angelic beings. We also know that satan and his fallen angels were thrown out of heaven to the earth. So there are two kingdoms at play here, the Kingdom of God and the Kingdom of Darkness. Satan lost the war in heaven, which means he has now declared war on the believers of Jesus here on earth. We are direct reminders of all that satan hates. Many times we are taught that Satan is defeated; this can be a half-truth. Yes, he has been defeated in heaven. He lost that war. But we must open our eyes and realize Scripture says that when satan lost that war, he was cast to the earth with great wrath. This does not describe a cowering defeated devil. It is a warning of a furious, vengeful, bitter, and hateful army of demons. Hell-bent on destroying all that God has called good.

It is a dangerous belief and teaching to say that satan is defeated here on earth. This pacifies believers and creates a naive church. This opens many up to involve themselves in demonic realms and activities without realizing it. It fills churches up with people learning behavior modification and not a genuine change of heart and mind. This belief system creates a lazy non-combative way of serving the Lord and just waiting to die and go to heaven. This is not true. I'll go as far as to say that it is a tactic used by satan to convince the world he either doesn't exist or, at the very least, is a pacified enemy waiting for judgment. I am sorry to inform you that we are at war. The Kingdom of Darkness is here, and we are the ones behind enemy lines.

Before the cross, satan had access to heaven. Yet, the rules of heaven did not apply to him. He was not of heaven; he was from his Kingdom of Darkness. So in a way, we can say that satan was an ambassador of his kingdom. We all know that an ambassador can go into another nation and not be bound by the rules and laws of that nation. He is not a citizen of that nation. He is there for one reason: to represent his kingdom and set up an embassy in the foreign land. This is why all of heaven rejoiced when satan and his demons were cast out. Satan was no longer given access. He was now bound to his kingdom on earth. Then the Word of God through the Apostle Paul said something powerful.

2 Corinthians 5:20 *Now then, we are ambassadors for Christ, as though God were pleading through us: we implore you on Christ's behalf, be reconciled to God.*

In the past, satan was the ambassador as a representative of his Kingdom of Darkness. Now the tables have been turned. Scripture now says that we are ambassadors. We are representatives in a foreign land. We do not belong to this wicked kingdom. We are not of this world. The rules and laws of the Kingdom of Darkness do not apply to us. We live according to the kingdom we represent. We are called to set up embassies in this foreign land and plead and implore others to change citizenship. This is our duty, job, and assignment.

Let's dive into a few Scriptures that talk about the Kingdom of God.

Matthew 4:17 *From that time Jesus began to preach and to say, "Repent, for the kingdom of heaven is at hand."*

Matthew 12:28 *But if I cast out demons by the Spirit of God, surely the kingdom of God has come upon you.*

John 18:36 *Jesus answered, "My kingdom is not of this world. If My kingdom were of this world, my servants would fight, so that I should not be delivered to the Jews; but now My kingdom is not from here.*

Luke 9:1-2 *Then He called His twelve disciples together and gave them power and authority over all demons, and to cure diseases. 2 He sent them to preach the kingdom of God and to heal the sick.*

Matthew 10:5-8 *These twelve Jesus sent out and commanded them, saying: "Do not go into the way of the Gentiles, and do not enter a city of Samaritans. 6 But go rather to the lost sheep of the house of Israel. 7 And as you go, preach, saying, 'The kingdom of heaven is at hand.' 8 Heal the sick, cleanse the lepers, raise the dead, cast out demons. Freely you have received, freely give.*

Let's summarize a few facts from these few verses.

- Jesus felt it necessary to preach repentance.
- Everywhere Jesus went, He stated that the kingdom of heaven was there
- Jesus said that His kingdom is not of this world. It is from a different place
- Jesus gave disciples the power and authority over demons and to cure diseases
- Jesus sent the disciples to preach the Kingdom of God and to heal the sick

At first glance, a few things might stand out that don't seem to be related. For instance, why was Jesus so adamant about preaching that the Kingdom of God was here and to have authority over demons and to heal the sick. Let's break this thought down. In the fallen world, there is sickness, disease, death, pain, and wickedness. This is the place we are born into. This is the description of the Kingdom of Darkness. But Jesus was not of this place, and because He rose again, neither are we. But, of course, we need to anchor this in Scripture. Here it is.

Colossians 1:13 *He has delivered us from the power of darkness and conveyed us into the kingdom of the Son of His love.*

Definition of Conveyed: transport or carry to a place.

The above verse unequivocally shows that Jesus has delivered us from the Kingdom of Darkness. And it uses an interesting word, 'conveyed.' We have been transported and carried to another place. The Bible says that we are in heavenly places in Christ Jesus. How can this be if we are still in the flesh on earth? This can only be done with the Holy

Spirit. Our soul has been intertwined with the Spirit of Christ. If Jesus is in heaven, and a part of Him dwells within us. Then by default of our Savior, we are also in heavenly places. What happens in the Kingdom of God happens with us.

The Kingdom of God is the opposite of the Kingdom of Darkness. In God's Kingdom, there is no sickness, no pain, no death, no disease, and wickedness. Remember, if we are ambassadors, then the laws of our Kingdom apply to us no matter where we set up our embassy. So if we are ambassadors, then the embassy is our place of worship, our church, our living room, our jail cell. Any place two or three are gathered, Jesus is there in the midst. This is powerful! Think of the Lord's prayer that so many recite without even realizing what they are saying.

Matthew 6:9-13

9 In this manner, therefore, pray: Our Father in heaven, Hallowed be Your name. 10 Your kingdom come. Your will be done On earth as it is in heaven. 11 Give us this day our daily bread. 12 And forgive us our debts, As we forgive our debtors.13 And do not lead us into temptation, But deliver us from the evil one. For Yours is the kingdom and the power and the glory forever. Amen.

Reread verse 10; really read it. Look at what it is saying. That God's kingdom comes and His will be upon this earth in the same way it is in heaven. So what is the Lord's will? I'll show you.

2 Peter 3:9 *The Lord is not slack concerning His promise, as some count slackness, but is longsuffering toward us, not willing that any should perish but that all should come to repentance.*

This Scripture shows us that it is not God's will that any should perish. That any be lost. Also, the Lord's will is the great commission. That we disciple the whole world. The Lord's will is also that we lay hands on the sick and cast out demons. In the same way, He wants His kingdom to be manifested to the world through His ambassadors. Through us! We are to show those trapped in the Kingdom of Darkness that they can be free, healed, and delivered.

When Jesus came to this earth as a human, He left all power and authority in heaven. He did not cheat at being a human. He got tired like we do, hungry as we do. The nails hurt in the same way they would hurt us. The whipping, the crucifixion, was precisely what we would feel. So many get it mistaken and think He somehow cheated and operated in powers that only He could operate in. NO! He came as a complete human to show us what we can do. This is why He prayed to the Father, to show us. This is why he said; greater things will you do than me. He operated on this earth through the power of the Holy Spirit, which we also have. In the spirit, we can step into the throne room of God in boldness. Because Jesus lives in us. He is the King, the Prophet, and the High Priest. This is why we can lay hands on the sick and command the body to be healed. Because we bring the Kingdom of God and manifest it in the lives of others, that is why Jesus said to preach that the Kingdom of God is at hand. When someone is healed, it is a direct manifestation of a different kingdom.

14

THE CHURCH AND THE KINGDOM

In this chapter, I want to distinguish the difference between the Church and the Kingdom of God. Let's begin with the definition of the word Church.

Ecclesia, Greek Ekklēsia – An assembly of people. A gathering.

The word 'Church' that Jesus used was a Greek word that meant a group or gathering. The church was never meant to be defined as a building. Nor was the word 'Church' ever meant to be one single person. I know it's a very popular saying these days, especially to those who don't like attending a church gathering to say, "I am the Church." That is just as incorrect as those that believe the church is a building or cathedral. A Church is a gathering of people. This does not mean that it has to be dozens or hundreds of people. But one cannot be alone and declare that they are the church. There is a reason God created different gifts and talents. We all need each other to work as the body of Christ. A single human body part cannot function as a body, and neither can we as the body of Christ.

When Jesus came to preach the Kingdom of God, He had to establish ground here on earth. Jesus, Himself said to Pilate that His Kingdom was not here on earth.

John 18:36 – *Jesus answered, "My kingdom is not of this world. If My kingdom were of this world, My servants would fight, so that I should not be delivered to the Jews; but now My kingdom is not from here."*

This is very key in understanding the importance and position of the church. This is why I continually use the term embassy. An embassy is simply a representation of a nation or kingdom. It is a building that represents a foreign nation. When we put the 'Church' in its proper position and context, we can see how the 'Church' is crucial in God's eyes.

Every single gathering of believers is a heavenly stronghold within the Kingdom of Darkness. In this light, we can see why it is so vital for order, holiness, rightful judging within the assembly of people. Every 'Church' must represent its Kingdom to the best of its ability to compel others to leave the Kingdom of Darkness and become citizens of the Kingdom of God. Each believer, each church is a living brochure for the Kingdom of God.

When a 'Church' is not put in its proper position and context, things go wrong each time. Many times the 'Church' is lifted as the center. Almost a Kingdom unto itself. This kind of thinking, by default, becomes a competition with other embassies (churches). It creates a race to become the biggest embassy, the fanciest, most respected, and known. The ambassador (Leader) becomes the focus instead of Jesus. This is dangerous for many reasons. The root of this is pride. We know that pride is what brought satan down and kicked out of heaven. We must run from this at all costs.

I want to share something the Lord showed me when reading the story of Jesus in the gospel of Matthew.

Matthew 4:8-10 *Again, the devil took Him up on an exceedingly high mountain and showed Him all the kingdoms of the world and their glory. 9 And he said to Him, "All these things I will give You if You will fall down and worship me."*

10 Then Jesus said to him, "Away with you, Satan! For it is written, 'You shall worship the Lord your God, and Him only you shall serve.'"

Even though I had read this passage, I discussed this passage many times for many years. Sometimes we need to learn not only to see what is written but also what is not written. What jumped out at me is the fact that Jesus did not argue with the devil about his reign over all the kingdoms of the world. The devil could never offer Jesus all of the world's kingdoms unless he were the rightful owner. We know that Satan is the god of this world according to Scripture. Because Satan is the god of this world, then by default, every kingdom in this world is owned by the god of this world.

In the same way, a business person can own an entire block. So by default, every business that opens within that block is under the ownership of the business person. Why is this important? This should be very important to every pastor, preacher, teacher, and ministry leader.

When a pastor builds his own personal kingdom, he is the rightful king of that kingdom. Jesus ceases to be the King in that building. It is no longer an embassy to the Kingdom of God. This can be a pastor, an evangelist, a teacher, or even a committee. Please hear me when I say that many churches may look the same, but there is a clear non-compromising difference. Any place of worship will either be its own kingdom, or an embassy, a representation of the Kingdom of God. No church can be both. Many are against church buildings and instead grow house churches, yet this can also be another kingdom built on pride and therefore default as a kingdom of this world.

When we have defined the church building as the center, we can also lead many to lose faith. For example, churches worldwide are burned down, destroyed, closed-down, fall apart or decay to a few families that eventually die away. So if we exalt the embassy, what happens when the embassy is overrun?

For instance, our embassies of the United States have been attacked, destroyed, bombed, and overrun. Is this a huge loss? Yes, it is. But when an embassy falls, this does not cause the Kingdom that the embassy represents to fall. So those that are around do not lose heart when an embassy falls. Because the Kingdom still reigns and will build again. Look at this Scripture in Hebrews.

Hebrews 12:28a *Therefore, since we are receiving a kingdom which cannot be shaken,*

Brother and sister, please understand that we belong to a Kingdom, not an embassy. Because embassies can be shaken, but the Kingdom of God cannot. I love pastoring a church in a church building. Not only do I love it, but I know I've been called to do it. A person not called to the ministry in which they are operating will never last without the calling. Yet even though I am called, I never mistake the embassy (church) for the main focus. Jesus and His Kingdom will always be the focus. I am just an ambassador, just as yourself if you are a believer in Christ. Men, you are the ambassadors of your home. Women, you are the ambassadors over your family. Never forget that the ambassador's sole job is to represent the Kingdom where they belong.

Another crucial point that needs to be made is that Jesus is the head of the church. Yes, we all know this by memory, but do we believe it? I say that because so many bash the church. I know and understand that many who claimed to be the church have hurt, caused pain, destroyed, abused, and broken many. This, of course, leads back to the previous pages on two types of churches. But the true church was and is established by Jesus Himself. So let's go back to the time of Jesus to get a better grasp of this truth.

In the Bible, Jesus and His disciples were walking north of Israel to Caesarea Philippi. It was an ancient Roman city located in a cave with a spring in it, where the Jordan River began—flowing south through all of Israel. Many believed this was the birthplace of the god Pan, who was illustrated as a person with horns, ears, and legs of a goat. Surrounding the spring and cave was a massive rock on both sides of the cave. Over time, many gods were carved into the rock. This became a place of idol worship and child sacrifice. In the time of Jesus, Caesarea Philippi represented everything wicked and vile. The cave and spring were even recognized as the gates of Hades or the gate to the underworld.

This walk with Jesus leading must have been very confusing to the disciples as they followed. Why would Jesus be walking to the most wicked places in all of Israel? I sometimes wonder if the disciples looked at each other nervously as they got closer to their destination. Each one was nudging the other to ask Jesus why they were there. It was at this most wicked place that Jesus had one of his most important proclamations in history. So before I share the text, let me set the stage here. Jesus is standing there with the massive rock with carved idols looming over them. The sound of the spring can be heard; the place they all knew was the gates of hades. They could only imagine how many babies were thrown into the cave as a sacrifice to an idol. Then Jesus begins to speak. So let's go to the passage.

Matthew 16:13-19 *When Jesus came into the region of Caesarea Philippi, He asked His disciples, saying, "Who do men say that I, the Son of Man, am?" 14 So they said, "Some say John the Baptist, some Elijah, and others Jeremiah or one of the prophets." 15 He said to them, "But who do you say that I am?" 16 Simon Peter answered and said, "You are the Christ, the Son of the living God." 17 Jesus answered and said to him, "Blessed are you, Simon Bar-Jonah, for flesh and blood has not revealed this to you, but My Father who is in heaven. 18 And I also say to you that you are Peter, and on this rock I will build My church, and the gates of Hades shall not prevail against it. 19 And I will give you the keys of the kingdom of heaven, and whatever you bind on earth will be bound in heaven, and whatever you loose on earth will be loosed in heaven."*

We read a fascinating conversation between Jesus and His followers. In that wicked place, standing on that demonic rock, Jesus asks them who do people say that He is. This then leads to some interesting answers. For example, some disciples said that many thought Jesus was John the Baptist, or Elijah and many other prophets. Then Jesus directs the question even closer. He must have looked each of them into their eyes and asked, "Who do you say that I am?" Wow, what a powerful question. I still believe the Lord asks this of many today. Unfortunately, many professed Christians still see Him as simply a teacher, suggesting a way to live. Others see Him as King but never as Lord of their life. I imagine the disciples stood there, not knowing how to answer. Finally, after a moment of silence, Peter speaks up. "You are the Christ, the Son of the living God." This is a powerful statement. Surrounded by idols that don't speak or walk, Peter declared that Jesus is the Son of the living God. So it was vital to differentiate a dead god compared to the living God. Peter was declaring that all other gods were dead. Something dead has no power. This was when Jesus made the incredible statement that still causes my heart to stir. Amid the rock full of idols and the cave that many called the gates of the underworld, Jesus said, "On this rock, I will build my church." This is a declaration of war.

Let me explain. In ancient times kingdoms would war against each other. When one kingdom defeated the other, it was very important to show the defeated nation that they were defeated. The best way to do this was to build their temples over the temples of the defeated nation. This would demoralize them and was a statement that the defeated nations' gods were not strong enough against the winning nation. This is why religious sites are layered when excavated. Each time a new nation came, they would build on the ruins of the defeated nation. So when Jesus said on this rock, I will build my church. It was a declaration of war against everything demonic that the rock represented. For all we know, He pointed at the giant rock and said those words. I will conquer, I will defeat, I will dismantle and win. I will build my Church on this rock as a show of defeat over all that Satan has built. The Church belongs to Jesus, and we are a part of it. Together is the only way we will function as the church should in this world. Praise Jesus for his declaration. Jesus is Lord.

15

IDENTITY OF JESUS CHRIST

As we dive into the identity of Christ, I feel it necessary to talk about a few things first. One of these begins with a question.

Have you ever wondered why we don't read about demonic manifestations before Christ?

In the book of Psalm 106:35-37 (AMP) *But they mingled with the (idolatrous) nations and learned their ways, 36 And served their idols, which became a (dreadful) snare to them. 37 They even sacrificed their sons and their daughters to demons.*

In reading this passage, we can see that the people of Israel mingled with nations that worshipped idols in the Old Testament. This caused the chosen people to learn wicked ways, even to the point of sacrificing their sons and daughters to demons. Please note that Scripture sees idols as demons. This is what is behind every false god in this world. There will always be a demon behind each one. In the times of the Bible, there were many of these idols/demons. Here is a list of a few.

- Molech
- Baal
- Dagon
- Ra
- Ashtoreth
- Chemosh
-

The many gods are countless, depending on which tribe, nation, and continent. Between the fall and the birth of Christ, this world fell into the domain of satan. Our earth became his Kingdom of Darkness, and he set high ranking fallen angels over regions and principalities. Each demon prince was named, with many of them worshipped as gods. There was no reason for demons to manifest or possess humans if he already owned them. The entire world was enslaved by sin and dominated by Satan.

All of this was threatened when Jesus was born. This is why satan caused Herod to kill all of the children two years or younger in Bethlehem. Satan knew what the Scriptures prophesied of the coming Messiah, but he is not all-knowing. I imagine he and all of his fallen angels were on the lookout for the coming Messiah. I believe this is why he caused so many in Israel to worship idols; what better way to stop the Messiah from coming than by destroying the very nation that would birth Him. Jesus was about to dismantle the Kingdom of Darkness once and for all completely. Scripture describes it like this.

John 1:1-5 *In the beginning was the Word, and the Word was with God, and the Word was God. 2 He was in the beginning with God. 3 All things were made through Him, and without Him nothing was made that was made. 4 In Him was life, and the life was the light of men. 5 And the light shines in the darkness, and the darkness did not comprehend it.*

The Kingdom of Darkness had so oppressed the World that it would not comprehend the light of Jesus. It was unthinkable, unimaginable. Jesus was about to cause the Kingdom of Darkness to tremble.

Matthew 3:1-2 *In those days John the Baptist came preaching in the wilderness of Judea, 2 and saying, "Repent, for the kingdom of heaven is at hand!"*

In talking about the identity of Christ, we also must talk a bit about John the Baptist. He was a forerunner in letting the nation of Israel know that the Messiah was coming. Not only the Messiah but a new kingdom. He began preaching near the Jordan River and compelling the people to repent of their sins. To turn away from their old life and be baptized. All for the purpose of ushering in a new kingdom. For the sake of clarity, let's go over a bullet-point list from creation to the time of John the Baptist.

- Man falls into a sinful nature and is infected for all generations
- Man loses authority and identity
- Satan reigns
- Demons are worshipped
- Satan has access to the throne room of God to accuse
- The Kingdom of Darkness was established
- There's a threat of a new kingdom

Jesus said something so unique about John the Baptist.

Luke 7:28a *For I say to you, among those born of women there is not a greater prophet than John the Baptist.*

Wow! Why would Jesus say that John the Baptist was the greatest prophet ever? John never opened the Red Sea. John never marched around a city seven times and watched it tumble down. John never spoke prophetically about the coming Messiah. John never called fire down from heaven or stopped it from raining for years. Maybe we scale prophets according to the works that they did. Could it be that God sees things differently than ourselves? Let me share something with you. The greatness of a prophet is not based on anything else other than the greatness of his message. In other words, God judges how great a prophet is by how great his message is. What prophet carried a more important message than preparing the way for Jesus? This leads us into the identity of Jesus. We learn a lot by knowing that satan wanted to kill Jesus as a baby. We also learn that the greatest prophet was considered great because he spoke of Jesus. This speaks volumes as to who Jesus is. Also, all of the demons being worshipped were about to be threatened by a greater kingdom than theirs. So let's find out more about Jesus through the following passage.

Luke 4:31-34 *Then He went down to Capernaum, a city of Galilee, and was teaching them on the Sabbaths. 32 And they were astonished at His teaching, for His word was with authority. 33 Now in the synagogue there was a man who had a spirit of an unclean demon. And he cried out with a loud voice, 34 saying, "Let us alone! What have we to do with You, Jesus of Nazareth? Did You come to destroy us? I know who You are – the Holy One of God!"*

We can learn a lot about the identity of Jesus. Verse 32 says that the people were astonished at the teachings of Jesus because His words were with authority. This does not mean Jesus yelled louder than any other teacher or rabbi. They had heard many people teach before, but none spoke like Jesus. There was a stirring that happened each time He spoke. So we learn that Jesus' teachings were dripping of authority. And all of that authority was confirmed in the next few verses. A man was in attendance in the synagogue, and in the middle of Jesus teaching, the demon within the man couldn't stay quiet. So the devil and his demon partners began to scream out. Even the demons know that Jesus spoke with authority. Even to the point that the demons began to beg Jesus. Thinking He was there to destroy them. This is also a great insight as to the identity of Jesus. They admitted that Jesus could destroy them. This is an important revealing because only God can have complete authority and power to destroy devils. We see something similar happen in another passage.

Matthew 8:28-29 *When He had come to the other side, to the country of the Gergesenes, there met Him two demon-possessed men, coming out of the tombs, exceedingly fierce, so that no one could pass that way. 29 And suddenly they cried out, saying, "What have we to do with You, Jesus, You Son of God? Have You come here to torment us before the time?"*

Once again, we see an example of demons showing their weakness by begging for Jesus not to torment them yet. This is interesting. This means they know there will come a time where they will be tormented. There is no doubt in their fear of Jesus. This again points to the fact that only God can destroy demons or send them to be tormented. These demon-possessed men were so dangerous that nobody dared walk through their territory. Yet we see Jesus walking through their domain, and the demons themselves feared Jesus. So here is another similar passage.

Luke 4:41 *And demons also came out of many, crying out and saying, "You are the Christ, the Son of God!" And He, rebuking them, did not allow them to speak, for they knew that He was the Christ.*

In this passage, we learn that Jesus even had the authority to command demons not to speak. We also see that they cried out. So, in summary of these few passages I shared, we know without a shadow of a doubt that Jesus is the Messiah, God manifested in the flesh. He has the power to shut demons up and the power to send them to be tormented. They know He is the final judge and the Christ, the anointed Son of God.

To add to this, Jesus fulfilled every single prophecy in the Old Testament pertaining to the Messiah. The weather obeyed Him; sickness obeyed Him; demons obeyed Him. He was the one spoken of by Moses, Isaiah, Jeremiah, and many more prophets. God manifested in the flesh. The light in a dark world.

Once Jesus was crucified, buried, and resurrected, all power and authority were upon Jesus.

Matthew 28:18 *And Jesus came and spoke to them, saying, "All authority has been given to Me in heaven and on earth.*

This is a very bold statement that only God Himself could ever say without it being blasphemy. Not only did Jesus claim to have all authority in heaven, but also on earth. This is a literal sentence. There is no other way to interpret it. It is plain and straightforward that Jesus holds all authority. This could only mean one thing. That Jesus is the image of the invisible God. The Lord spoke to Abraham, Moses, and all of the prophets, kings, and priests. All things were created for Him and by Him. Jesus was there in the beginning.

John 1:1-5 *In the beginning was the Word, and the Word was with God, and the Word was God. 2 He was in the beginning with God. 3 All things were made through Him, and without Him nothing was made that was made. 4 In Him was life, and the life was the light of men. 5 And the light shines in the darkness, and the darkness did not comprehend it.*

This is the identity of Jesus. He is Lord of all Lords and Kings of all Kings. Praise be to Jesus, the lamb of God who takes away the sins of the world.

16

OUR IDENTITY

Every previous chapter has all been written to get to this point. The question of who are we? We do have to come to grips with this fact first. Jesus did not come to fix your old self; He came to destroy it. So many times, we make the mistake of thinking we can serve Jesus in our old self. This is impossible. This is made clear in Scripture.

Mark 2:22 *And no one puts new wine into old wineskins; or else the new wine bursts the wineskins, the wine is spilled, and the wineskins are ruined. But new wine must be put into new wineskins."*

This example was given in Scripture to teach that we can never put something new into something old. In the days of the Bible, the new wine was still fermenting, and if put into an old wineskin, the gases would cause it to explode. New wine had to be put into a new wineskin. We are the same when we come to Christ. So the Lord will not patch up your old man. He will first make you new.

2 Corinthians 5:17 *Therefore, if anyone is in Christ, he is a new creation; old things have passed away; behold, all things have become new.*

When we surrender our lives to the Lord, He makes us new. Old things pass away. We are no longer rooted in Adam and sin. Instead, the Lord pulls us out of the Kingdom of Darkness and brings us into His Kingdom. As believers, this is the hardest part to live out. It can take a lifetime for the renewing of the mind. What the Lord does, He does it instantly. Many make the mistake of saying they are under construction as if the Lord is slowly making you new. This is a lie of the enemy. What God does, He does right away. Once the Lord does this change within us, our minds now need to catch up and be renewed. This is why we must read our Bibles! It is the only way to renew our minds indeed. There is a spiritual washing when we read our Bibles—each time renewing old lies with truth. So let's look at another Scripture about what happens when we surrender our lives to the Lord.

Ezekiel 36:26-27 *I will give you a new heart and put a new spirit within you; I will take the heart of stone out of your flesh and give you a heart of flesh. 27 I will put My Spirit within you and cause you to walk in My statutes, and you will keep My judgments and do them.*

This Scripture gives us a clear understanding of a repentant heart. It's a promise that the Lord will provide us with a new heart, that our old heart, made of stone, will be replaced. That He will then put His Spirit within us to cause us to walk correctly in the ways of the Lord. We cannot do it unto ourselves. The filling of the Holy Spirit, which is the new wine, must be poured in to replace the old. When the Lord pours His Holy Spirit into us, He does not do this in portions. The Holy Spirit is a person, so can this be portioned out? The Holy Spirit does not come in pieces but as a person. We can never come to the Lord of ourselves. We can never worship the Lord, read our bibles with understanding, or live a new life without the Holy Spirit. The moment we have a true surrender to the Lord, the Holy Spirit comes into our new heart made of flesh.

This is the part many misunderstand. Once a new believer comes into the kingdom, many are told they need to worship harder and pray harder for the Holy

Spirit to come into their lives. They do not understand that a heart can never change without the indwelling of the Holy Spirit. Many may testify the day they surrendered to Christ and a different day they spoke in tongues. So they automatically share that they must have been saved, and the day finally came when God finally poured in the Holy Spirit, almost as if they had to make themselves worthy first. This is not what I see in Scripture. The gospel is many times described as a seed. We all know that seed never stays a seed once it is buried. Instead, a seed is put into the dirt; water is added that causes the seed to germinate. This begins a reaction, and the seed starts to grow roots and a stalk that will eventually bust through the dirt and be visible.

1 Peter 1:23 *having been born again, not of corruptible seed but incorruptible, through the word of God which lives and abides forever*

Brother and sister, when you surrender your life to the Lord completely, He puts an incorruptible seed within you. The Holy Spirit indwells within you completely. We now have to water that seed to anchor, grow roots and finally bust through the flesh so all of the world can see. When this spiritual stalk grows to the point of getting past our flesh, it is evident. Some will speak in tongues; many will show a boldness like never before. Others will begin to feel words of knowledge bubble out of nowhere for those we pray for. The gifts of the Spirit will start to show in your life. We cannot stop there. We need to continue to water what is growing through the Word of God. There is no special anointing on some. God is no respecter of men. Meaning God does not show favoritism within His children.

Acts 10:34 *Then Peter opened his mouth, and said, Of a truth, I perceive that God is no respecter of persons:*

What many mistake as a special anointing is simply one that waters the seed of God more. We, as believers, must never focus on growing the plant into a giant tree for everyone to see. This is an error dipped in pride. Our focus should always be to grow roots deeper into Christ. A tall tree is only as strong as its roots. This is why many known ministers fail and fall into a scandal. Their hearts turn prideful, and they do all they can to grow their tree for all to see. Yet, the roots are shallow, and the tree will eventually fall.

In the same way, never focus on the fruit. I have met so many that want the fruit for others to see.

This is backward. A fruit not attached to the vine is impossible. When you walk into a fruit stand, we are amazed at how beautiful the fruit looks. In actuality, all you are looking at is dead fruit. It no longer receives nourishment. It is no longer attached to its lifeline, the branch. In a short time, all of that fruit will begin to rot.

In the same way, never focus on the spiritual fruit in your life. Instead, be focused on being attached to the vine, which is Jesus. When you are permanently attached to the vine, the fruit will always come forth. It is automatic. The nourishment is continual; therefore, the growing fruit is continual.

One other thought I'd like to share about fruit before we continue. When fruit is left on the tree for too long, it will eventually wither and fall. Fruit is meant to be picked and eaten by others. It is intended to nourish and bless those that are around it. The tree does not worry about losing its fruit because it knows it will continue to make more. The only reason a tree would want to withhold all of its fruit is once again pride. To look beautiful to others. This is an error and demonic. The spiritual fruit the Lord gives us is not for us. It is not to exalt ourselves. The fruit is to nourish all of those around us. Our gifts of the Spirit are for others to grow and be blessed. Our blessing is the fact that we are attached to the vine, which is Christ. Our roots are in Christ, and that means life. Our fruit is never too hoard. Hoarded fruit will only wither, fall and die. One could never hold on to their fruit any more than a tree holds onto its fruit. It is better to feed others than allow them to die. When this happens, nobody receives the blessing.

Not the tree or those who are around it. Let me end this paragraph with this illustration. Imagine a giant field on a farm. The kingdom of God is the field, the water that gives growth is the Word of God, and the sun that causes growth is the Lord. The seed is that which is put into our hearts. We are the branches that will stay strong and grow for as long as we are attached to the vine. Jesus came to be the one that tends to the fruit. He pulls out the weeds; He destroys all of the parasites that are trying to kill us. A tree needs the sun, but let's turn the letter u to an o. It is not the sun but the Son that causes us to grow. Thank you, Jesus.

I want to share some verses that speak truths about our identity in Christ. These are key and need to be anchored into our hearts.

Colossians 3:3 *For you died, and your life is hidden with Christ in God.*

This verse lets us know that our old man is dead if we are in Christ. We cannot live as believers through our old man. This is not possible. Those that try to live a life as a believer without becoming new is simply behavior modification. There is a beautiful, powerful promise and statement in the above verse; It states that we are hidden in Christ. If one is hidden in Christ, then how can this world affect you. How can demons attack you if you are hidden in Christ? To those now in Christ, a part of your identity is that your old self is dead, and you are hidden in Christ. This is a fact according to Scripture. Let this become an anchor that holds you amid storms.

ANCHOR

- Your old person is dead.
- You are hidden in Christ.

Galatians 2:20 *I have been crucified with Christ; it is no longer I who live, but Christ lives in me; and the life which I now live in the flesh I live by faith in the Son of God, who loved me and gave Himself for me.*

This is another powerful scripture that we need to anchor into our hearts and minds. Paul states to the region of Galatia that he has been crucified with Christ. The cross always meant death. So once again, we see that we are new. Our old self is crucified. Dead to this world and dead to sin. Paul continues by saying that it is no longer he who lives but Christ in him. According to this Scripture, we now no longer live for ourselves. In everything I do, it is to please God. The words that I speak, the deeds that I do should not be me. It is Jesus who lives in us. This not only pertains to sin; this pertains to ministry. I will not pray for the sick through me because I am dead. I will lay hands on the sick as Christ who lives in me. I will command demons to come out through Christ who lives in me. I will not preach of my own words but through Christ who lives in me. If we continue in verse, we come to the understanding that Paul is not crazy. Paul is not literally saying that we are robots and no longer ourselves. He understands that while we are here on earth, we are living in our flesh. So even though our flesh weakens us, Paul states that we need to live it out through faith in Jesus.

ANCHOR

- Your old person is crucified with Jesus
- You no longer live for yourself
- It is Christ who lives in you
- While in this life, we live through faith in Jesus.

Colossians 1:19-23 19 *For it pleased the Father that in Him all the fullness should dwell,* 20 *and by Him to reconcile all things to Himself, by Him, whether things on earth or things in heaven, having made peace through the blood of His cross.* 21 *And you, who once were alienated and enemies in your mind by wicked works, yet now He has reconciled* 22 *in the body of His flesh through death, to present you holy, and blameless, and above reproach in His sight—* 23 *if indeed you continue in the faith, grounded and steadfast, and are not moved away from the hope of the gospel which you heard, which was preached to every creature under heaven, of which I, Paul, became a minister.*

There is much to explain about this passage, but I urge you to take your time to make it an anchor in your Christian walk truly. First, let's look at it one verse at a time. In verse 19, it reveals an important truth. An entire book can be written about this very subject. I will do my best to summarize. It says it pleased the Father that in Him (Jesus) all the fullness of God should dwell. The Bible does say that Jesus is the image of the invisible God. When you and I go to heaven, we will not see the Father and Jesus as two separate persons. There are not two or three thrones in heaven. To see God visibly is to see Jesus. This Scripture pleased the Father that all of God, every attribute, power, honor, and glory should dwell in Jesus. All power is given unto Jesus.

In verse 20, we know it is a continuation from verse 19 because verse 19 ends with a comma. This verse lets us know that through Jesus, all things have been reconciled. To reconcile is to bring something together.

Reconcile – to restore to friendship or harmony b: to settle or resolve (differences) 2: to make consistent or congruous

So in reaching verse 20, it lets us know that Jesus came to restore, settle and resolve our predicament because of Adam and the fall of humanity. Jesus came to make things right. The verse also lets us know how He did this through the blood He shed on the cross. This was the only way to restore our right standing with God. Jesus created the bridge by becoming the bridge through the shedding of His blood. As you read this, you might think to yourself that you already know these things. Yet, we cannot stop there. All of this builds up to the following passage. This verse describes in what way we needed reconciling in the first place. Verse 21 says that we were alienated, which means separated, isolated, and withdrawn. Yes, ever since the fall of Adam, we have been separated from our creator and isolated from Him. This is exactly what satan wanted. And the worst part is that the enemy has convinced us that God was our enemy. Yet the verse clearly says that we were enemies in our minds. God was never your enemy. We were lied to and manipulated that God wanted nothing to do with us.

The fact that we were enemies of God in our minds has got to be the greatest lie that Satan has ever used. Imagine for a moment a loving family with a baby. This baby was loved and nurtured with compassion. The baby had the coziest crib and welcoming home. Every day the parents would show their love by caring, feeding, and keeping the baby safe. Then one day, the baby was abducted and taken away. The kidnappers then took the baby and locked it into a cold basement. It was given no blanket or pillow. The baby was thrown crumbs and leftovers to eat. For years the baby grew up in the basement, in complete darkness. The abductors continually told the child that it was ugly, stupid, dumb, and not worth anything. Finally, the child grows up and knows only darkness, dampness, and cold concrete. It learned to eat molded crumbs off of the floor. Suddenly one day, a man comes to rescue the abducted person. They are taken out of the darkness and brought back home, back to the warm cozy home. The now-adult is showered with love and mercy. They are given a meal and sit at the table. But the person has never eaten from a plate using utensils. They instantly throw the plate to the ground and eat the food off of the ground. They are taken to their bedroom with a soft mattress and warm blankets. But the person does not know how to receive such things and sleeps on the floor. They are told that they are precious and beautiful, but they do not believe it because they were told it was ugly and stupid for all of their life. The person screams to the rescuer, "Why did you save me! I'm not worth saving!" This is the lie your abductor has told you and me. This is why we must believe what God says about us rather than ourselves. We have been lied to. We are worthy of saving. We need to begin to see ourselves through the eyes of God. We are only His enemy in our own minds. We can never truly walk in our identity until we get past the lies the abductor (satan) has told us. Satan is a liar, a manipulator, a thief, and a destroyer. You do not rightfully belong to your abductor. Jesus died on the cross two thousand years ago to rescue you once and for all from the clutches of the enemy. God brings us into His Kingdom, where we rightfully belong. But what good is it to sit at the Lord's table if we continue to throw down what He is serving us, only to eat off of the floor like an animal? No! You are more precious than anything He has created. You were the lost lamb, and He has found you. He rejoices because you are no longer in the abductor's basement surrounded by darkness. You have been re-planted into His Kingdom and surrounded by His glorious light.

Let's continue to verse 22. This is also a huge anchor to place into your heart so that you may be grounded in Christ. That way, no matter what storms life may bring, you will stay steady. This verse presents three powerful words about how we stand in the eyes of Jesus. It says God presents us holy, blameless, and above reproach. Let's look at each of these words.

- Holy – this means set apart. Holy is not a super-spiritual word that is beyond comprehension. It simply means to be set apart. So, according to this verse, the Lord sets us apart from the world. When one is married, and you share your vow with your spouse, you make yourself holy unto that person. You are setting yourself apart from all others. You will only be for the person that is standing in front of you. We do the same with God. He sets us apart to no longer be used by satan. We are holy, set apart for God and God alone.

- **Blameless** – Not only are we set apart for God, but we are blameless. This is what the enemy loves to do. To add shame, guilt, condemnation, and fear to us. Yet the Lord says that He throws our sins away as far as the east is from the west. That He will throw our sins into the deepest ocean and allow them to be buried. In the eyes of God, we are blameless. Satan wants us to blame ourselves for being in darkness, but God knows better. God knows that we were stolen, abducted, and lied to. This is why God can have mercy on the sinner. When we come to Christ and surrender our hearts, He finds us blameless. How moving it is to accept in your heart that God sees you blameless indeed. This is freedom, my friend. This truth is what breaks the chains of sin that we are weighed down with.

- **Above reproach** – I enjoy this word. In the past, before the cross, Satan was allowed to accuse mankind day and night. This word is a legal term that means we are above accusation. Satan can no longer accuse us. It is not admissible in the courts of heaven. Any guilt, shame, condemnation has to be struck out of the records. You cannot be called by what you were in the past. This is why our old man must be crucified with Christ. Our new man is above reproach, above accusation. When we realize that we are holy, blameless, and above reproach, renew our minds with this truth. You will see the powerful manifestation of God in all that you do.

The following passage speaks for itself, and I will share it and summarize it.

Romans 6:1-11 *What shall we say then? Shall we continue in sin that grace may abound? 2 Certainly not! How shall we who died to sin live any longer in it? 3 Or do you not know that as many of us as were baptized into Christ Jesus were baptized into His death? 4 Therefore we were buried with Him through baptism into death, that just as Christ was raised from the dead by the glory of the Father, even so we also should walk in newness of life. 5 For if we have been united together in the likeness of His death, certainly we also shall be in the likeness of His resurrection, 6 knowing this, that our old man was crucified with Him, that the body of sin might be done away with, that we should no longer be slaves of sin. 7 For he who has died has been freed from sin. 8 Now if we died with Christ, we believe that we shall also live with Him, 9 knowing that Christ, having been raised from the dead, dies no more. Death no longer has dominion over Him. 10 For the death that He died, He died to sin once for all; but the life that He lives, He lives to God. 11 Likewise you also, reckon yourselves to be dead indeed to sin, but alive to God in Christ Jesus our Lord.*

This passage takes all we have learned and again reiterates the truth that we are dead to our old selves and now live in Christ. We are no longer rooted in sin. To say you are a follower of Jesus and continuing to claim that you are in sin is a slap to the face of Jesus. Jesus came to undo what the first Adam did. So, in essence, if we surrender our lives to the Lord yet still claim to be in sin. What we are saying is that Adam's fall is still stronger than the crucifixion of Jesus. How can Jesus come to undo what Adam did, yet the majority of the church still claims to be rooted in Adam? Let me put it simply with a question.

Who is stronger, Adam or Jesus?
What is stronger, sin or the blood of Jesus?
Do you genuinely believe Jesus came to undo what Adam did?

This leads us to the conclusion that Jesus is stronger than Adam; the blood of Jesus is stronger than any sin. And if Jesus came to undo what Adam did, then I am no longer under the curse of sin. I have died to Christ, and it is Christ who lives in me. This truth breaks the chain's bondage; it breaks the self-doubt that has defeated us time and time again. We have been set free from the hold of sin, and while we are in the flesh, we believe we will continue to defeat sin by having faith in Jesus.

According to verse 6, we are no longer slaves to sin. According to verse 9, death no longer has dominion. Jesus was the first to rise again. The fact that Scripture says Jesus is the first means there will be a second, a third, and so on. Jesus defeated death, and so will all those that surrender their lives to Jesus. Our flesh will die someday, but we will close our eyes to this world and open them in His Kingdom.

17

THE GREAT COMMISSION

In case you don't know, the Great Commission is a passage in the Bible. To be more accurate, it is what we consider the Lord's last commandment before He ascended to heaven. So let's read it together.

Matthew 28:18-20 *And Jesus came and spoke to them, saying, "All authority has been given to Me in heaven and on earth. Go therefore and make disciples of all the nations, baptizing them in the name of the Father and of the Son and of the Holy Spirit, teaching them to observe all things that I have commanded you; and lo, I am with you always, even to the end of the age."* Amen.

To thoroughly read this in context, we need to understand that this is not a suggestion from Jesus.

It is a direct order and commandment to those that believe in Him. With the resurrection of Jesus, all authority now belongs to Him. Not only on earth but also in heaven. This is a heavy, powerful statement for Jesus to make. So please make no mistake about it. Jesus did not suffer on the cross, undo what the first Adam did to ascend and sit on a throne for nothing to change here on earth. Instead, he came to take back the authority that was stolen from Adam. I believe most Christianity believes this part wholeheartedly. The next part of the passage is either ignored, misunderstood, or not taken into consideration. When Jesus says the words, "Go, therefore." This is Jesus handing to believers the 'deed' that was stolen from Adam. Jesus is once again the holder of the deed, and He gives us the authority that rightfully belonged to us. To have dominion over every creeping thing on this earth. Well, guess who is bound to this earth? Yes, Satan and his fallen angels. This automatically puts demons underneath us. Because we come in the name of the Lord Jesus, we are operating in His authority.

In the same way, a police officer operates under the badge of their city. They do not have authority unto themselves, but once the badge is put on, they can now speak, give out a ticket, or arrest under the authority given to them as police officers. Jesus commands us to use that authority He suffered and died for and make disciples everywhere we go. Teaching all to observe and learn all that Jesus taught. So let's look at another passage written by Mark.

Mark 16:14-18 *Later He appeared to the eleven as they sat at the table; and He rebuked their unbelief and hardness of heart, because they did not believe those who had seen Him after He had risen. 15 And He said to them, "Go into all the world and preach the gospel to every creature. 16 He who believes and is baptized will be saved; but he who does not believe will be condemned. 17 And these signs will follow those who believe: In My name they will cast out demons; they will speak with new tongues; 18 they will take up serpents; and if they drink anything deadly, it will by no means hurt them; they will lay hands on the sick, and they will recover."*

Once again, we see the Great Commission. Jesus gives a command to go to all of the world and preach the gospel. The gospel is the good news that all can be freed from the bondage of sin. That Jesus came to set the captive free. This should always be our focal point in reaching others for Jesus. Our goal should never be to add more church members; it should bring the lost to Jesus. Then Mark goes into greater detail and mentions signs. Demons being cast out, speaking in new tongues, serpents will not harm you, poison will not harm you, and laying hands on the sick for recovery. In this passage, we need to notice more than these signs is the fact that Jesus said these signs would follow those that believe. We should never follow the signs. This can quickly become idolatry or pride. The signs flow from the root to the fruit and never from the fruit to the root. These signs from God come naturally in the same way a well-watered tree grows fruit. Walk in your God-given authority against our true enemy. Jesus deserves His rewards. If you do this, you will be able to witness the power of God manifested here on earth as it is in heaven. Let's look at another passage.

Luke 24:46-49 *Then He said to them, "Thus it is written, and thus it was necessary for the Christ to suffer and to rise from the dead the third day, 47 and that repentance and remission of sins should be preached in His name to all nations, beginning at Jerusalem. 48 And you are witnesses of these things. 49 Behold, I send the Promise of My Father upon you; but tarry in the city of Jerusalem until you are endued with power from on high."*

Once again, we can see that it is important to Jesus

that we be witnesses for Jesus. Since we are called to be witnesses, we need to make sure we know what it means. So what is the definition of witness?

Definition of witness – one that gives evidence, one who has personal knowledge of something, something serving as evidence or proof

So, according to the definition, we need to have personal knowledge of Jesus. This is only possible through a relationship with Him. Also, how can we witness unless we witness the power of God through the signs that follow His believers? This way, we can speak out of confidence from evidence and proof of God's power. The gospel is not just a friendly suggestion or poetic literature. There is power in the name of Jesus, and when we proclaim Him, the signs are evidence that what we are saying is true.

1 Thessalonians 2:12 *that you would walk worthy of God who calls you into His own kingdom and glory.*

Many people on this earth have high expectations expected of them: Doctors, judges, police officers, pastors, and political leaders. According to the verse above, this also goes for all believers in Christ. We are representatives of Jesus and His Kingdom. We need to walk worthy of the calling on our lives. The Great Commission is not something to take lightly. Do you realize most reject Jesus because of the example set by those that claim to follow Jesus? We need to walk worthy of God. When a pastor fails, this sheds a bad light on those pastors that are not failing. When a police officer fails, it sheds a bad light on the entire police force. This cannot be for something so much more important.

The Bible says in Luke 12:48

But he who did not know, yet committed things deserving of stripes, shall be beaten with few. For everyone to whom much is given, from him much will be required; and to whom much has been committed, of him they will ask the more.

A commitment to Jesus is so much more than crying at an altar and saying a few words in prayer. It is a commitment, a surrender, a letting go. We cannot serve two masters. When the gospel is shared freely, we must never believe salvation has no value; this is a disservice to the Lord. Therefore, we need to be able to share the beauty of God's forgiveness without cheapening it. Emotions are good, they are given to us by God, but we cannot solely follow Jesus through emotion alone. This also goes along with the next verse.

2 Corinthians 5:20 *Now then, we are ambassadors for Christ, as though God were pleading through us: we implore you on Christ's behalf, be reconciled to God.*

We must never forget that we are ambassadors for Jesus. It is not about us; it is about Jesus. All we do in word and deed reflects on the one we represent. This is an important position for each believer to have. This is why we must disciple, teach and admonish one another. The better we equip each other, the better we will all be. An ambassador mindset will not feel competition with other ambassadors. Competition becomes an issue when the ambassador wants to build up their kingdom here on earth. We need to be intentional in our mindset that our focus and only assignment is to bring the lost to the feet of Jesus. Each time we minister to the lost, the broken, the wicked, and the possessed. We can never forget where we came from. We need to remember that we also were bound by sin and wickedness. We also were unable to save ourselves. Never forget your humanity and weakness when you speak to others. Remember the undeserving mercy you received from the Lord, yet He still died for you.

Jesus delivered us from the power of darkness and brought us into His Kingdom. So we then need to share this news and solidify it, manifesting the power of God in their lives in whatever way the Holy Spirit leads. At the end of it all, all believers in Christ will reign with Him. But only a few will demonstrate the power of the Kingdom of God here on earth. That can be you, beginning now.

Colossians 1:13-14 *He has delivered us from the power of darkness and conveyed us into the kingdom of the Son of His love, 14 in whom we have redemption through His blood, the forgiveness of sins.*

18

HOW DO I APPLY THIS TO MY LIFE?

Many times I have taught believers their identity in Christ. It encourages them, sets them free. I can see the excitement in their eyes for the future. Then as the days pass by, the excitement dies. This teaching never truly became a part of their daily Christian life. Everything goes back to normal, and it becomes another great teaching to add to their closet of teachings in their mind. I don't want that to happen. While I can't be there by your side to walk this out, I can write this chapter in getting over the hurdle of some practical ways to pray for others for healing or deliverance. To be honest, this chapter could be a book unto itself, but I will try to do my best to help you walk in your identity in Christ. Also, please remember, this teaching is never to be used to exalt yourself. The entire body of Christ needs to learn so they too can move in the power of the Holy Spirit. Remember the Bible says that in the last days, I will pour out my Spirit upon all flesh. Gone are the days that evangelists and preachers exalt themselves as they fly personal jets to big auditoriums so thousands can watch them. Gone are the days where they teach us that they alone are special and anointed, so we need to follow them to the point of idolatry. We, the church, are anointed; we are called to do great and mighty things. We are the ambassadors of Christ, and we will bring heaven to earth so all can see. I will be describing different scenarios with how to possibly handle situations. Remember, as you grow and become more accustomed to operating in your identity in Christ, these things will become yours. You will find your way through your character and personality.

Commanding healing: When someone has pain or is sick and asks for prayer, Jesus said in the Bible.

Mark 11:22-24 *So Jesus answered and said to them, "Have faith in God. 23 For assuredly, I say to you, whoever says to this mountain, 'Be removed and be cast into the sea,' and does not doubt in his heart, but believes that those things he says will be done, he will have whatever he says. 24 Therefore I say to you, whatever things you ask when you pray, believe that you receive them, and you will have them.*

Never in this Scripture does Jesus tell us to ask Him to move the mountain. Jesus was straightforward in saying to have faith in God and speak to the mountain. When we command healing, we are not commanding God to heal. We can never command God to do anything. What we are commanding is the person's body. Remember, we have been given authority by Jesus Himself to all that is on the earth. The flesh of a person is under that same authority. We are not begging, asking, or suggesting for the pain or sickness to leave. We are commanding. Not in our name or our power, but the power and name of Jesus Christ. A person is not the body of flesh; that is simply the vessel for the soul. A person's soul is who they truly are—their personality, character, and everything about them. Our soul will live forever; our flesh will not. Our flesh is bound to this earth, and once we pass, it will become dust. So never mistake a sickness to belong to that person. It is simply the vessel of that person.

Satan knows we live in a fallen world. In a fallen world, horrible things happen. There is starvation, murder, disease, pain, and aging. Our flesh is the bridge that allows us to live in a physical world. For our soul to live here on earth, it needs a vessel, our body. So as long as our body is here on earth, it will be hurt, sore, feel pain, get disease and become sick. This will always be the point of contact that the enemy can and will attack. Demons cannot attack you because you are hidden in Christ. But your flesh is here. If you believe that you are a body that happens to have a soul, you will be fighting demons all the days of your life. But, in reality, you are a soul that happens to have a body. This is key in understanding. This is why we have to renew our minds.

Romans 12:2 *And do not be conformed to this world, but be transformed by the renewing of your mind.*

We need to conform our thinking from this world to the Kingdom of God. We need to stop living this life through our flesh and cause it to submit to our spirit and soul. I know this might sound challenging, but in time it will become natural to live supernaturally.

So now that you understand that we are commanding the body to fall into submission, then your mindset is that healing will manifest. Jesus paid the price, and He deserves His reward. I will ask the person just to receive and not pray. I will either lay my hands on the area of pain if appropriate or just hover my hand over it. I will NOT make it about my words, a long prayer, or long eloquent poetry of commands. I will make it simple and allow the Holy Spirit to do what He does best. I will not get in His way. I know I am simply a conduit for the Holy Spirit to pass through. I am not waiting for healing to fall from heaven. I know Christ lives in me, so whatever I touch is also what Jesus touches. And we know that if Jesus touches anything, pain or sickness cannot be there. So then I will say something simple. Here is an example.

"Lord, I thank you for all that you do. I speak to this pain; I speak to this sickness and command it to be restored and healed. I command all pain to leave in Jesus' name. I serve an eviction notice to this sickness and command it to leave now. In Jesus' name. Amen."

I say these words and leave my hand there. Allow the Spirit of God's power to flow through you to that person. Sometimes a few seconds, sometimes up to a few minutes. It's okay at this point to ask them if they feel anything. Many times they will feel a shift, or heat, or tingling. If a specific body part hurts when moved, ask them to move it. This part is essential. Eight out of ten times, the healing will come after the person moves the hurting part. My only conclusion for this is that it takes faith to move what was hurting. Faith moves the healing to be manifested.

Do I have to touch the person?

No, you do not have to touch the person physically. I have prayed for healing over the phone or a Zoom call. I have prayed for healing as I preached on the pulpit, and a person sitting in the back of the building received healing. Our job is not to figure out how God does it but to be an ambassador and speak out what the Lord is speaking in. For example, if a female asks for prayer, I will often hover my hand over her head or ask my wife to put her hand on the woman. We are always to conduct ourselves appropriately.

Do I need to use praying oil for healing or deliverance?

No, we must never attach our faith to items because this causes a crutch. So what happens if you do not have oil to pray? Unfortunately, many churches believe healing is like a lottery ticket. Maybe, just maybe, if we pray loud enough, worship loud enough, run around the building enough, speak in tongues enough, that maybe, just perhaps, a healing will come down. These things only block the flow of the Holy Spirit in the sense that it makes us believe the setting has to be perfect.

Am I saying that healing or deliverance from demons does not happen in these settings? No, I am not. I know for a fact that many have been healed in these settings. What I am saying is do not allow yourself to believe that this is the only way the Lord can work. These things cause a belief system. And when we build a belief system like this, it creates a dam where the Spirit of God cannot flow.

I do not want to have a belief system that healing only happens when a worship team is blaring or healing oil is poured. I believe that the Holy Spirit is always present and willing to touch a person's body. Whether in a church building or an alley. Have I been requested to use healing oil? Yes. Do I use it on them, yes? A few times, I am about to pray for someone for healing, and they take out a bottle of oil. I do not go into profound teaching about such things. Instead, I simply take the bottle, put some oil on my hand, and command healing. Why would I do this? Because I know that this person is sick or in pain, they have already built a belief system that healing requires oil. There is nothing wrong with healing oil, so I use it. Even fluctuation of voice can hinder a person's healing because of their belief systems. Maybe they have seen healings in a pentecostal church setting where the preacher is commanding at the top of his lungs.

I have commanded healing for someone in a quiet voice in a church lobby once, and as I commanded, no healing came. I knew the person's background and quickly realized they felt my prayer wasn't fired up, so therefore, how could they be healed. I did not argue or laugh. I simply prayed again a little louder and commanded in the name of Jesus for the pain to leave. Guess what happened? Yes, the pain left. We, humans, are an interesting peculiar creation. Thank God that He realizes how we are built and how our minds work. Jesus will honor our faith by whatever capacity our faith reaches.

Is it okay to ask how much pain they are in?

Yes, many times, I do ask them on a scale of 1 to 10. I do this because the healed often don't realize they are healed if the pain subsides but does not entirely go away. I do not always ask this unless I feel it is necessary. Many times healing is not instant and takes place over minutes or even a day. So by asking them to gauge it, faith can arise in their hearts as they feel the pain go down on the scale. So be careful when asking what is causing the pain. When someone says cancer or a severe illness, this can cause you to be discouraged. Jesus told us to speak to the mountain, but these mountains often become bigger and bigger as the person shares about their sickness. I once prayed for a person's leg, not realizing it was a disease since birth. Once they were healed, the person shared with me about their illness. I was floored because had I known before commanding healing; I honestly would have been discouraged. As we mature in commanding healing, we will learn to grow in faith to the point that previous mountains will begin to shrink.

What if the person says the pain shifted in their body?

In my experience, many times, this is demonic oppression. Pain does not shift. If you hurt your knee, and someone is praying for your knee, the pain will not make a sudden shift to a shoulder. At this point, you need to stop commanding for healing and begin to command that spirit of pain and trauma to leave immediately, in Jesus' name.

How do I build up my faith for healing?

This will only happen while doing it. It is the same with learning to ride a bike or a car. In the beginning, you are nervous; you overthink things and become rigid. Only over time of driving or riding a bike can you allow yourself to relax. This is the same. The more you do it, the better it will become with greater results. Does one fall off a bike and never get back on again? No, you dust yourself off and ride again. I will say this, and this is key. You need to allow your faith to grow; this will only be done by seeing the power of God move. The more healing you see, the more faith rises, which then allows you to see more. Faith builds upon faith to the point that you will be surprised not to see the power of God manifest in healing.

Can I pray more than once for healing? Yes, Jesus Himself prayed twice for a man to see.

Mark 8:22-25 *Then He came to Bethsaida; and they brought a blind man to Him, and begged Him to touch him. 23 So He took the blind man by the hand and led him out of the town. And when He had spit on his eyes and put His hands on him, He asked him if he saw anything.*

24 And he looked up and said, "I see men like trees, walking."

25 Then He put His hands on his eyes again and made him look up. And he was restored and saw everyone clearly.

Why didn't healing happen?

There are many reasons, but please never let a cause be that you didn't do your part. Jesus says to lay hands on the sick, and they shall recover. The recovering part belongs to the Lord; our role is laying hands on the sick. We need to live out of obedience. We do live in a fallen world, and in a fallen world, we still die. I have prayed for many in the ICU; some are healed, others go to be with the Lord. This is a reality in this world.

Please keep this thought in your mind. Do all get saved that you share the gospel with? No, yet you should not discontinue sharing the gospel of Jesus Christ. We need to do the same. We share the gospel out of obedience; we pray for the sick out of obedience.

Can someone lose their healing?

Yes, this happens, and I believe it can be for many reasons. One of the most common reasons is that the person continues to open the door for that sickness. For example, suppose a person is healed from lung cancer but continues to smoke. Or if a person is suffering from heart disease yet does nothing to be healthier after their healing. God has given our bodies to us, and we need to be good stewards of this body. It is the only body we are given, and we must care for it.

I prayed for my family member who I love, and nothing happened?

I have seen this many times. I believe what happens is when we command healing over someone we love very much, We get in the way of the Holy Spirit. We become a blockage. This could be because we are so broken that we pray to see the person healed out of our own will. Or it could be that the person knows us so well, they can't see Jesus in you. This then does not allow them to receive. If this happens, have someone you know outside of the family to command healing. So many times, this is what finally breaks the sickness, and the person is healed.

Does the person being prayed for need faith?

No, many times, we need to pray for a child,

someone in a coma, or a non-believer. The person being prayed for will be healed out of your faith. In the Bible, Jesus raised many from the dead. There was no way for the deceased to have faith. In the same way, build yourself up in your faith. Once they are healed, their faith will rise.

Why do more non-believers get healed than believers?

Many times this is a sad truth. I believe it is a cause for a few reasons. Unfortunately, many Christians are full of doctrine and belief systems that block the Holy Spirit from moving in their bodies. For generations, we have been taught that healing is more of a lottery win than something the Lord gives freely to all who ask. It is similar to the paralyzed man near the pool of Bethesda.

John 5:1-8 *After this there was a feast of the Jews, and Jesus went up to Jerusalem. 2 Now there is in Jerusalem by the Sheep Gate a pool, which is called in Hebrew, Bethesda, having five porches. 3 In these lay a great multitude of sick people, blind, lame, paralyzed, waiting for the moving of the water. 4 For an angel went down at a certain time into the pool and stirred up the water; then whoever stepped in first, after the stirring of the water, was made well of whatever disease he had. 5 Now a certain man was there who had an infirmity thirty-eight years. 6 When Jesus saw him lying there, and knew that he already had been in that condition a long time, He said to him, "Do you want to be made well?"*

7 The sick man answered Him, "Sir, I have no man to put me into the pool when the water is stirred up; but while I am coming, another steps down before me."

8 Jesus said to him, "Rise, take up your bed and walk." 9 And immediately the man was made well, took up his bed, and walked.

Christians have been wrongly taught that maybe, just maybe, if they have a church service that is fired up. Perhaps if the anointing is just right that someone will get healed, this is the same belief that the man had, waiting for an angel to stir the water to be healed. This story is in the Bible for a reason. To show us today that this is not how healing works.

Another reason non-believers are more often healed is the simple fact of Jesus' love. Throughout the New Testament, we see that wherever Paul took the gospel, the signs followed. This caused many to believe in Jesus. The Holy Spirit will always move in power as a co-signing of the message being shared.

Casting out a demon

One important thing I cannot stress enough is that demons are liars. Please do not build doctrines by what demons say or have said to others. I have heard so many teachings on deliverance and casting out demons built on things demons say while being cast out. So please let this truth be a part of your walk. Never believe demons. Let's look at what Jesus says.

John 8:44 *You are of your father the devil, and the desires of your father you want to do. He was a murderer from the beginning, and does not stand in the truth, because there is no truth in him. When he speaks a lie, he speaks from his own resources, for he is a liar and the father of it.*

If Jesus says the devil is a liar, then I believe it. There is no argument about this truth. So there is no reason for me to have a conversation or debate with a demon that refuses to come out. Every demon must submit to the Holy Spirit within us. I am not going to attempt to write a chapter on casting out demons in an exhaustive way. This would require an entire book on different situations, testimonies, and problems. But I will share a few thoughts that will help you when confronted with anything demonic.

Do I have to be a believer?

Absolutely yes. A non-believer or a carnal Christian can deal with demons, but it can be dangerous. Demons are not afraid of Bibles, crosses, holy water, or a church building. There is one thing that will cause a demon to tremble, Jesus. When we know who we are in Christ, the very blood of Jesus becomes our covering. His Holiness is our holiness. His anointing is our anointing, and His authority is our authority. Let's look at a passage from the book of Acts when non-believers tried to cast out a demon.

Acts 19:13-17 *Then some of the itinerant Jewish exorcists took it upon themselves to call the name of the Lord Jesus over those who had evil spirits, saying, "We exorcise you by the Jesus whom Paul preaches." 14 Also there were seven sons of Sceva, a Jewish chief priest, who did so.*

15 And the evil spirit answered and said, "Jesus I know, and Paul I know; but who are you?"

16 Then the man in whom the evil spirit was leaped on them, overpowered them, and prevailed against them, so that they fled out of that house naked and wounded. 17 This became known both to all Jews and Greeks dwelling in Ephesus; and fear fell on them all, and the name of the Lord Jesus was magnified.

When I command a demon to come out, it is not my command; it is the Lord's. Therefore it is none of my business to require a conversation with a devil. I am given an order from God, and I will execute it. Jesus died for every person on this planet, and Jesus deserves His reward.

Think of it like this. Your father owns a house, and someone trespasses the home and makes it their own. You happen to drive by the house and notice that trespassers are living in it. You saw the blood, sweat, and tears your father worked to buy that house. He paid a high price. You should feel a righteous desire to make things right. So you get the paperwork, bring a police officer, and knock on the door. Now imagine the trespasser opening the door and refusing to leave. What do you do at this point? Do you speak kindly and ask them why they are there? Do you sit on the couch and have a conversation with them? Maybe they've been there over 90 days, so now they feel ownership of the house. Do you suggest that they get out? Or do you show them the deed to the house and demand that they leave? I would tell them they need to get out; my eviction notice is the Bible itself and will not take no for an answer. Jesus paid for each person on this earth, so every demon is a trespasser. It doesn't matter what story they have or what reason they have. So they must pack up and go in the name of Jesus.

Do demons come back once a person is delivered?

Yes, many times. Praise God there are ways to prevent this from happening. So let's look at Scripture.

Matthew 12:43-45 "*When an unclean spirit goes out of a man, he goes through dry places, seeking rest, and finds none. 44 Then he says, 'I will return to my house from which I came.' And when he comes, he finds it empty, swept, and put in order. 45 Then he goes and takes with him seven other spirits more wicked than himself, and they enter and dwell there; and the last state of that man is worse than the first. So shall it also be with this wicked generation.*"

When I have seen demons come back, it is usually because the person delivered continues to open doors to the enemy or never truly wants them to leave. I have seen demons delivered from a person, only to come back once the person that prayed deliverance leaves. This is done often. A person that does not renounce will usually stay with those demons. This is not every time, but often enough to deem it necessary to write in this book.

There is only one sure-fire way to have them delivered for the rest of their lives with this truth. That is, bring them to Christ. Walk them through surrendering their lives to Jesus. If a demon manifests, do not argue, instead cast it out. Demand that it leave immediately in Jesus' name. Once the devil or demons have left, continue walking them through salvation. Once they repent and make Jesus their Lord and Savior, pray over them, command all demonic doors to be closed that were once open. Command anything ungodly to leave and not come back. Command any demonic stronghold to be broken and scattered in Jesus' name. Have the person agree with you each step of the way. Demons feel they legally belong in the person, so the person must agree with your prayers to make it legally binding. This person must be discipled to grow in Christ each day.

Should I be with someone when casting out a demon?

If possible, always have someone with you,

especially if the person is of the opposite sex. This is highly important. A man should never be alone to cast out a demon from a woman, or vice versa. This is never appropriate! Jesus sent His followers in groups of two to cast out demons and lay hands on the sick.

Luke 10:1-2 *After these things the Lord appointed seventy others also, and sent them two by two before His face into every city and place where He Himself was about to go. 2 Then He said to them, "The harvest truly is great, but the laborers are few; therefore pray the Lord of the harvest to send out laborers into His harvest.*

What if a possessed person won't look at me?

Often, a demon will not come out and will cause the person to shield their eyes from you. Instead, command this person to look at you as you demand that demon goes in Jesus' name. The demon is simply procrastinating from leaving.

Do demons sometimes manifest as a sickness in a person's body?

Yes. We can see this clearly in Scripture.

Luke 13:10-13 *Now He was teaching in one of the synagogues on the Sabbath. 11 And behold, there was a woman who had a spirit of infirmity eighteen years, and was bent over and could in no way raise herself up. 12 But when Jesus saw her, He called her to Him and said to her, "Woman, you are loosed from your infirmity." 13 And He laid His hands on her, and immediately she was made straight, and glorified God.*

Many things stand out in this passage. First, let's walk through it to learn the truths in it. We know that Jesus often healed the sick that came to Him. In this passage, we see a sick woman. Her back was bent forward, and she could not straighten herself up. This is nothing new to Jesus; I'm sure He had healed this type of sickness in other towns. One would think He would simply heal her as He did before. Instead, Jesus knew this was not just a sickness; there was a spirit of sickness that had the woman wrapped up. Instead, Jesus commanded her to be loosed by that spirit. Once the spirit was gone, Jesus laid hands on her to be healed, and her back was now straight.

Many demons are in agony and pain from the many battles with angels. These demons will then attach themselves to a person, and the demon's pain will manifest in that person. Many times a doctor will not find anything wrong. A specialist will do every test imaginable and find nothing. This demon of pain and sickness must leave in Jesus' name.

I will end this chapter with two powerful tools the church has been given for deliverance. Unfortunately, the church has not used these tools and made them merely symbolism. This is having the power but denying the power thereof. We, as the church, need to get back to the basics of moving in the power of the Holy Spirit.

WATER BAPTISM –

So many times, I have witnessed water baptisms with only half of the reason taught. Water baptism is a symbol, yes, but so much more. It is a symbol that just as Jesus was buried, we are buried in the water. Just as Jesus rose again, we rise again out of the water. We are a new creation and with God and our family and friends as witnesses to our baptism. These are all beautiful things to say and witness. But we must not miss the most powerful part of this act.

The Bible states in Romans 6

Romans 6:1-17 *What shall we say then? Shall we continue in sin that grace may abound? 2 Certainly not! How shall we who died to sin live any longer in it? 3 Or do you not know that as many of us as were baptized into Christ Jesus were baptized into His death? 4 Therefore we were buried with Him through baptism into death, that just as Christ was raised from the dead by the glory of the Father, even so we also should walk in newness of life.*

5 For if we have been united together in the likeness of His death, certainly we also shall be in the likeness of His resurrection, 6 knowing this, that our old man was crucified with Him, that the body of sin might be done away with, that we should no longer be slaves of sin. 7 For he who has died has been freed from sin. 8 Now if we died with Christ, we believe that we shall also live with Him, 9 knowing that Christ, having been raised from the dead, dies no more. Death no longer has dominion over Him. 10 For the death that He died, He died to sin once for all; but the life that He lives, He lives to God. 11 Likewise you also, reckon yourselves to be dead indeed to sin, but alive to God in Christ Jesus our Lord.

12 Therefore do not let sin reign in your mortal body, that you should obey it in its lusts. 13 And do not present your members as instruments of unrighteousness to sin, but present yourselves to God as being alive from the dead, and your members as instruments of righteousness to God. 14 For sin shall not have dominion over you, for you are not under law but under grace.

15 What then? Shall we sin because we are not under law but under grace? Certainly not! 16 Do you not know that to whom you present yourselves slaves to obey, you are that one's slaves whom you obey, whether of sin leading to death, or of obedience leading to righteousness? 17 But God be thanked that though you were slaves of sin, yet you obeyed from the heart that form of doctrine to which you were delivered.

In summary, the above passage lets us know that we are no longer bound to sin after baptism. Our old person has been crucified with Christ. Death no longer has dominion over us, and verse 17 states that we have been delivered. A demon is attached to our old man, our old person. Once that dead person is put to rest in the waters of baptism, it no longer has anything to hold onto. You are now hidden in Christ. In other words, you have left no place for the demon to attach itself. All doors have been shut, closed, and sealed by the blood of Jesus. When baptizing others, teach them this before going into the water. It does no good if this truth is not shared with the person being baptized. You want to share this truth and allow the seed to be buried. Many times when this is taught to a person, they come out of the water, manifesting. Cast that demon out, make sure there are none left, and pray for the person to instead be filled with the Holy Spirit.

COMMUNION – Here is another powerful tool that has been turned into mere symbolism. So let's go to the passage first.

Luke 22:17-23 *Then He took the cup, and gave thanks, and said, "Take this and divide it among yourselves; 18 for I say to you, I will not drink of the fruit of the vine until the kingdom of God comes."*

19 And He took bread, gave thanks and broke it, and gave it to them, saying, "This is My body which is given for you; do this in remembrance of Me."

20 Likewise He also took the cup after supper, saying, "This cup is the new covenant in My blood, which is shed for you. 21 But behold, the hand of My betrayer is with Me on the table. 22 And truly the Son of Man goes as it has been determined, but woe to that man by whom He is betrayed!" 23 Then they began to question among themselves, which of them it was who would do this thing.

In this passage, we can see that when Jesus takes up the cup, He says it is a new covenant. A covenant means an agreement, a contract. This is key and important because demons operate out of a legal system. They are soldiers of a wicked army and are very legalistic in nature. When Jesus says it is a new covenant, we need to explore that. There are covenants on earth that Jesus was replacing, such as the covenants of Moses. But in the spiritual sense, communion also breaks demonic contracts. Notice in the words of Jesus, He says in verse 20 that it is a new covenant in My blood. The blood of Jesus will always supersede any legality that demons believe they have over a person. If a person has been involved in witchcraft, occult, santeria, or anything demonic, this needs to be explained. Tell them that you would like to administer communion with them. Use bread and juice, any juice. Tell them that demons feel they have a right to them because of the doors they opened. Let them know that by taking communion, they agree that the blood of Jesus will void all contracts. Then take communion with them.

You do not need to be an ordained minister to give communion. Get a piece of bread and thank the Lord for the bread that represents His body. Ask the Lord to forgive you of any sins, whether knowingly or unknowingly. Ask the Lord to bless the bread and eat it. Thank the Lord after you eat the bread. Then take the cup of juice. Thank Him for shedding His blood on the cross. Thank Him for a new contract, a new covenant. The juice represents His blood in you. Ask the Lord to permeate every part of you in the same way the juice's nutrients will travel through your body. Drink the juice. Thank the Lord in Jesus' name for a new beginning. Amen.

I know there must be more questions than I could ever think to write and answer. I pray that this book has encouraged you and given you a new outlook on life. Learn to read your Bible through the lens of who you truly are in Christ. Learn to divide the old Testament from the new. Learn to discern Scriptures through your rightful standing in the Lord. Use this to uplift others and yourself. Use this to properly give Jesus the worship He deserves. Thank you, and God bless you. Let's destroy the strongholds of the enemy together in Jesus' name.

OTHER PARAKLETOS BOOKS

Made in the USA
Columbia, SC
21 December 2021